Jacobus de Ispania

The Mirror of Music
Book the Seventh

translated by
Rob C. Wegman

Lamotte

© 2017 Rob C. Wegman.
All rights reserved.

Jacobus de Ispania
The Mirror of Music
Book VII

<Contents>

Here begin the chapters of the Seventh Book of *The Mirror of Music*.

   1. Introduction to the Seventh Book of *The Mirror of Music*.
   2. What is measurable music.
   3. Wherefore discant is so called.
   4. What is discant.
   5. Which intervals are to be used in discant.
   6. Whether a fourth beneath a fifth is a consonance.
   7. That a fourth beneath a fifth is a consonance.
   <8.> Why the notes of the fourth concord better above a fifth than beneath it.
   <9.> Of foolish discantors.
   <10.> The difference between discants.
   <11.> What is tempus as it pertains to measurable music.
   <12.> How the previously stated description of tempus is being attacked by the moderns.
   <13.> That it is repugnant for tempus perfectum to be divisible into two equal parts.
   <14.> Confirmation of the things said.
   <15.> That division into whole parts is repugnant to the semibreve.
   <16.> Response to the counter-arguments.
   <17.> Defense of the ancients, and exposition of the things they said, as it touches upon the matter at hand.
   <18.> What is modus.
   <19.> How many modi there are.
   <20.> What is a note or figure of measurable music according to the ancients.
   <21.> The distinction of musical figures or notes according to the ancients.
   <22.> About the single figures which are called plicas.
   <23.> The distinction between long notes with respect to names and meanings according to the moderns.
   <24.> The distinction between the aforementioned notes with regard to certain shapes and degrees according to the moderns..
   <25.> That the duplex longa is not ligatable.
   <26.> That the duplex longa does not have a value of nine tempora.
   <27.> That it is irrational to notate a duplex longa which is called a larga.
   <28.> <That imperfect duplex longas are not necessary to this art.>
   <29.> That single imperfect longas of imperfect tempor are repugnant to this art, and likewise also songs put together from such imperfects.

<30.> That songs made from perfects are appropriately compared to the highest trinity.

<31.> That it is not necessary for a single longa to be equilateral.

<32.> That the imperfect breve is not necessary to this art.

<33.> Little prologue touching on the intention and the order of the things that are to be discussed.

<34.> That the moderns act irrationally in caudating semibreves.

<35.> <That if the semibreve is to be caudated, then this is less appropriate to the semibrevis minima than to the others.>

<36.> That if a singly-notated semibreve is to be caudated, then it must be done less inappropriately in obtuse angles rather than sharp ones.

<37.> That the semibreve is not to be notated by itself alone, without another semibreve or other [semibreves] next to it.

<38.> What the moderns say about the imperfections of musical notes.

<39.> What things are required for notes to either imperfect others or to be imperfected by them.

<40.> That one note may not imperfect another.

<41.> Response to certain conclusions that contradict the things said here.

<42.> To the insistence which can be the response.

<43.> Response to the second, fifth, sixth, seventh, and eighth conclusions.

<44.> Broader response to the things that touch upon the fourth, seventh, and eighth conclusions, together with a response to the ninth.

<45.> Comparison of the old art of measurable music to the new art with respect to perfection and imperfection.

<46.> Comparison of the old art of measurable music to the new art with respect to freedom and roughness.

<47.> Comparison of the old art of measurable music to the new art with respect to freedom and servitude.

<48.> Comparison of the old art of measurable music to the modern art, and of the old manner of singing to the modern one, with respect to stability.

<49.> Final conclusion of this work, and thanksgiving.

<Chapter 1. Introduction to the Seventh Book of *The Mirror of Music*.>

In his commentary to Aristotle's *Categories,* Simplicius says the following in praise of the ancients: *We are not altogether capable of distinguishing between truth and falsehood, but in this regard we choose to follow our betters.* Indeed, just as it is useful and praiseworthy to imitate things done well by the ancients, so it is pleasing and commendable to affirm, not contradict, the things they said well.

This seems to apply especially to the young, for although they are more eager to discover things, it is the elders who, for that very reason, should be proclaimed of better judgement by youths and novices who take pleasure in new things, according to this statement by Petrus Comestor: *although novelty is familiar and charms the ears, it does not follow that new things must be praised so much that old things be buried altogether* [*Hist. schol.,* Prol.].

Indeed, although many new teachings may shine outwardly at first sight, they often turn out, upon proper examination, to lack solid foundations within, are cast away, and do not last. Moreover, if *it is in vain* [to try] *to do with more what can easily be done with less* [Arist. *Phys.* 188a17–18], then what is the use of adding, to the good teachings of old, a frivolous and fanciful new doctrine, having rejected the former, when it is written: *Thou shalt not remove thy neighbour's landmark, which they of old time have set* [Deut. 19:14]?

In truth, *while* venerable men *have* formerly *dealt with plain music* [Franco, Prol.], such as Tubalcain before the flood, and thereafter many more whom we have recalled above, and [while] many also [have dealt] with measurable music, among whom stand out Franco the German and someone else called Aristoteles, now there have arrived, in our own time, novel and recent men treating measurable music, who have scant regard for their ancestors, the old teachers, nay rather, who in certain respects change, corrupt, reject, and destroy their good teachings in deeds (whatever they may profess in words), when it would be courtly and well-mannered to imitate them in well-said things, to excuse them in matters of doubt, and to expound them.

I, then, considering these things in their way of singing, and even more so in their treatises, was greatly saddened, and then I resolved to write down certain things about measurable music, with the first and primary intention of defending the ancients; thereafter, out of a secondary intention, I have tackled plain music and theoretical and practical music.

Having thus completed, with God's help, that which was accessory, let us now pursue, if we can, our primary purpose. And here indeed I seek a well-meaning reader: let him show consideration with me, let him, I plead, deign [to hear] me, for I am alone – which saddens me – and many are they against whom I undertake this last satyrical and polemical work. I do not doubt that the modern way of singing, and the treatises written about it, must be displeasing to many capable men; but I have not seen anyone who would write down something on the matter. I am now one of the ancients who are called backward by some. I am an old man. They are clever and young. Dead are they whom I uphold. Alive are they against whom I dispute. Those newcomers congratulate themselves on having found out new conclusions on measurable music. For me it suffices in this regard to uphold the old [conclusions], wich I consider soundly reasoned. For as [the moderns] say, citing from Aristotle in the Book of Meteors, *opinions and cycles of knowledge are* [always] *moving, for even where there is dry* [earth] *now, there was water before* [Muris, *Notitia artis musicae; De practica musicae*].

Nor let that which is done for love of Truth and, even more so, of devotion (for they, too, claim to be writing for love of Truth), be ascribed to presumption. *For if two friends exist, the most holy thing is to thoroughly honor the truth* [*Nic.Eth.* 1096a13–16]. *Socrates* [is] *a friend, but the truth a greater friend* [*Vita Arist.*]. Wherefore the blessed Jerome, citing Pythagoras, said in his Epistle against Rufinus: *Next to God, the Truth that must be cultivated is the only thing that brings humans close to God.* For he who forsakes Truth forsakes God, as God is Truth.

It seems respectful still to honor the ancients who grounded us in measurable music. It is respectful to uphold them in the things they said well, to expound them, not attack them, in matters of doubt. And it is uncivil and blameworthy to persecute good men who are dead, and who are unable to defend themselves. Let these things be said in my excuse. For although I shall say certain things against the statements of the moderns, [namely] where they counter the statements of the ancients, still do I esteem their persons. [For] I have loved song, singers, music, and musicians from the age of my youth.

<Chapter 2. What is Measurable Song.>

Measurable song is the appropriate joining together of different sounds that are equal or unequal [in pitch], and that are pronounced at the same time, under some measure of time.

Measurable song is related to plainsong, since both call for the appropriate joining together of different sounds that are equal or unequal. For "song" is, as it were, a genus in relation to plain and measured. Yet measurable song adds something to plainsong, namely, [the fact] that its different sounds are pronounced at the same time, and that [they are pronounced] under some measure of time, neither of which are requirements in plainsong. So three things, amongst others, combine to make measured song: the appropriate joining together of different sounds, their performance at the same time, and some sort of measuring of time in respect of them.

Now since the sounds in this kind of song are pronounced at the same time in order that some melodious sound may be born from them, it is necessary that the same unit of time be observed between them, so that the quantity held by one should be held also by the other.

The measurable art requires these and many other things, as mentioned above in Book I, Chapter 16. And song of this kind is called <measurable> because in it the different sounds are pronounced at the same time under some certain or uncertain interval of time. I speak of "uncertain" on account of *organum duplum*, which is not measured everywhere by a certain measure of time, as, for example, on the penultimates, in *fioraturae* where many notes in the discantus are sounding over one note in the tenor. Still, such song is classified under the measurable kind, since it involves discant, and it requires different sounds to be pronounced at the same time, sounds that cannot [all] be pronounced by one and the same person.

For measurable song requires several persons singing at the same time, and several parts, at least two or more. Consequently, although someone may sing plainsong by himself, as mentioned above, he cannot sing discant in measured song [by himself], which requires more things than does plainsong, as mentioned above, and as shall be mentioned below.

And since measurable song involves a certain discant, something must [now] be said about discant.

<Chapter 3. Wherefore discant is so called.>

Concerning discant, we must first consider and speak of it with regard to the matter of its name. Secondly, from these observations we must deduce what discant is, and what is the singing of discant. Thirdly, what are the more principal consonances to be used in discants. Fourthly, about foolish discants and [foolish] people singing discant. And thence onward to other things, as the matter may present itself.

As for the first, *discantus* is so named, in one interpretation, after *dya* which means two, and *cantus*, as it were two-fold song, or two songs, or a song of two, for although it may consist of more [than two], it is more proper for it to consist of two. And in the beginning there were perhaps no more than two parts in discant, that is, the one that is called *tenor*, and another which is sung upon the tenor and which is called *discantus*. But there is a difference between two songs and two persons singing. For there is no reason why there should not be more persons singing the two parts, the tenor as well as the discantus.

Since, therefore, the term *discantus* should apply more properly to two parts rather than more, one did speak in ancient times of *organum duplum*, in which there are only two parts. Thus the words used for *discantare* [to sing discant] were *organizare* or *diaphonizare*, for *diaphonia* is discant, as will be said below. And formerly it was proper for discant to be spoken of as [consisting] of two parts, since [the term] applies to the outermost notes of consonances that are blended and sung at the same time: for these [notes] are two and not more.

Alternatively one may speak of *discantus* after *dy* which means from, and *cantu*, as it were derived from chant, that is, from the tenor upon which the discantus part is founded, just as a building upon its foundation. That is why the chant is called *tenor* [holder], for it holds and provides the foundation for the discantus part. Who, after all, sings discant without a tenor, who builds without a foundation? And just as a building must be proportioned according to the foundation, in order that it be made not at the whim of the constructor but according to the requirements of the foundation, so the person singing discant must not sing the notes at his own whim but according to the requirements, and the proportion of the notes, of the tenor, in order that they be concordant with them. The discantus part, therefore, is dependent on the tenor, must be ruled by it, and must be concordant with it, not discordant. The tenor is not derived from the discantus part, but the other way round.

For the discantus notes can be placed against those of the tenor with which they must be concordant, and then such a part is called *discantus*. Alternatively they can be considered by themselves, not in relation to the tenor notes, nor in order that they be pronounced at the same time, yet separately and successively, one after the other, as when somebody sings some motetus, or some triplum or quadruplum, by itself, without a tenor and therefore not relative to anything. Such notes obey the rationale of chant. And one should speak of the tenor notes in the same way, either as they relate to the discantus notes and are pronounced at the same time, or as they are sung by themselves and separately.

Although it is more proper that there be one part to respond to one tenor, so that there are only two parts, it is possible to fashion more discants upon one tenor, such as motetus, triplum, and quadruplum. And when there is only one discant over the tenor, then one should observe more perfect and fewer concords, chiefly the fifth. But the more discants there are, the more concords may be used. For there may be many tenors that relate to many discants, though one of them must be the principal one. For when somebody makes the discant called triplum, he should watch not just the tenor notes, but also those of the motetus, in order that he makes concord with both tenor and motetus. And similarly, he who makes the quadruplum must seek his foundation in the notes of the tenor, motetus, and triplum. In this way, then, the tenor carries the rationale of both tenor and motetus in a three-part setting; and in a four-part setting, of tenor and motetus and triplum. And similarly beyond that, should there be more discants.

Let us now determine, from what has been said, what discant is.

<Chapter 4. What is discant.>

Under the name *diaphonia* Guido describes discant as follows: *Diaphonia is the separation of notes which we call organum, when the different notes sound apart in concordant fashion, and are concordant while sounding apart* [*Microl.* XVIII].

For *diaphonia* in Greek, *discantus* in Latin, is called after *dya* which means two, and *phonos* which means sound, as it were twofold sound, since it calls for different sounds to be pronounced at the same time. And this performing of sounds at the same time is commonly called *organum*, because *organon* in Greek is called *duplex modulatio* [double tune] in Latin, and because a human voice that is appropriately concordant and yet sounds apart, expresses the smoothness of the instrument called organ.

According to Guido, then, *diaphonia* or discant is called "the separation of notes which sound apart in concordant fashion, and are concordant while sounding apart," inasmuch as it calls for notes that are distinct or different, and yet blended together in concordant fashion, in such a way that what results is a separation because of the difference between the notes, and a conjoining because of the one-sounding quality of those notes in the concord. So it is not all separate or different notes that have a place in *diaphonia*, but only those that bring about a certain concordant sound when they are combined.

Master Franco, on the other hand, describes discant as follows: *Discant is a sounding-together of different parts in which those different parts are made proportionally equal through longas, breves, or semibreves, and are designated to be mutually proportioned by the appropriate figures in writing* [*Ars*, II].

Discant is called "the sounding together of different parts," because just as a sounding-together calls for different notes blended at the same time, so does discant [call for] different parts blended at the same time, and just as not any sounds blended at the same time bring about a blend that manifests itself smoothly and sweetly to the hearing, so not all different parts blended at the same time make discant, but only those which produce concord between them, in order that they make, through their good concordant sound, a song that sounds like it is one, even though there are more, just as the octave or fifth are made from different notes, and yet sound as one because of the good concord. When, therefore, someone makes discord with someone else, he is not properly singing discant.

What then is discant if not a song of two or more different parts, that sounds as one song because of good concord? To sing discant is to make a song from two or more different parts that sounds as one because of the smooth concordant sound. Or discantus is a part made upon a tenor that is different from it, yet [sounds] as one song because of the smooth blending of notes. To sing discant is to produce upon the tenor, or upon the tenor notes and simultaneously with them, other notes that are concordant with them.

So the person who sings discant is he who sings sweetly together with one or more [others] in order that from the different sounds may arise something that sounds as one, through the unity not of [actual] one-ness, but rather of the sweet and concordant blend.

<Chapter 5. Which consonances are to be used in discant.>

Discant, as is apparent from what has been said, is not to be put together indifferently from just any intervals, but only from those whose notes are concordant when pronounced at the same time. And according to Guido, there are three or four intervals that we [are to] use more chiefly, more often, and more confidently in *diaphonia* or discant, that is, the unison, the fourth, the fifth, and the octave. Thus he says in one place: *It should be known that three [intervals] are to be principally taken into consideration in all diaphonia* (that is to say discant), *namely, the octave, the fifth, and the unison.*

Elsewhere, however, rejecting the unison, he speaks thus: *There are three intervals which are to be chiefly used in* diaphonia, *namely, the fourth, the fifth, and the octave.*

These [intervals] *blend together into organum with such companionship and smoothness*, because of their good concord, *that they are called*, in a certain special way, *similitudes of notes and proper conjoinings of notes.* And he provides [the following] example of *diaphonia* made by means of those three consonances, using note signs fashioned from letters, though here in other figures, as follows:

Spera in Domino et fac bonitatem.
[Ps. 37: 3: Trust in the Lord and do good.]

In this example, the octave is formed by the outermost notes, that is, between the highest and lowest, the fifth by the upper and middle, and the fourth by the middle and the lower, and thus, in this example, Guido places the fifth above the fourth. This, however, goes against a certain modern teacher who states that the fourth is a consonance not below the fifth, but above [Muris, *Musica speculativa*]. And this matter shall be considered below. The said manner of discant is very simple, as it contains the same tune beneath and above and similarly in the middle, and a single note is sung against a single note. However, that the said three consonances are indeed the principal ones to be observed in discants is confirmed by Aristoteles, who speaks as follows when he describes discant:

> *Discant is song of certain different genera of two voices or three, in which only the consonant sound of three [intervals], that is, the fourth, the fifth, and the octave, obtains, being proportioned in natural fashion by the arrangement of long and short figures in accordance with the correct measure.* [Lamb. *Tractatus*]

Now although the said three consonances should indeed have pre-eminence in discants, at least as far as the consonances of unequal voices are concerned, one should not exclude many others whose notes, when mingled together, are concordant to a greater or lesser degree, which have been discussed above in the fourth book. For there are some notes that are more suitable for the singing of discant, and make more pleasing concordant sounds, than others. Unsuitable notes, however, diminish or augment the integrity of the octave or any other concord by some amount, and however small that amount may be, even if it is only a comma, they do corrupt that consonance, and destroy the concordant sound. Hence Guido says: *The dissonance of intervals that are derived by means of falseness creeps in into harmonious sound so badly that, when those who are too low diminish well-measured notes and consonances, or when those who move up beyond what is just <augment them>, they make the voices of men most hideous,*

As a discantus must therefore by its very nature make concordant sound with the tenor or tenors, it shall be the more perfect as it uses the more perfect concords. Provided, that is, that it shall be properly put together, for one should not use a good concord, or a better one, or even a very good one, all the time or too often, but rather alternately, now one, then another, according to the manner befitting the chant. Nor must the discantus always move up when the tenor moves up, or move down when it moves down, but rather move up when it moves down and move down when it moves up, though now and then, in appropriate places where the beauty of the chant allows it, the discantus may move down together with the tenor, or move up together with the same. For one must take great care that the beauty of the chant be maintained.

Three or four things appear to be needed, then, in order that discants be rendered praiseworthy and perfect: that there are good concordant sounds; that they encompass beautiful and well-composed musical sound, so much so that they are both pleasing by themselves and delightful for singing discant; and that they can be sung and measured with some ease.

At the present time, however, there are some discantors or writers of discant who pay no heed whatsoever to these conditions, who make discants without good concordant sound, who make wild songs that please badly, that are difficult, intricate, and almost unmeasurable, and thus they badly observe the four causes that are required in discants: the material [cause], in that they are concordant notes when produced together, the formal [cause], in that there is an appropriate arrangement, disposition, and composition of those things.

For concordant intervals do not suffice [by themselves] to make perfect and praiseworthy discant, unless they are well and appropriately arranged. And in order for this to happen, many things are needed which it would take a long time to explain each by itself. I am unable to satisfy all; this work occupies me much. But I say this in general that, just as *form lends existence* [Aquinas, *De ente et essentia*, IV], and a good and perfect form upon the right matter [lends] good and perfect existence, thus the proper arrangement of notes that are concordant between themselves produces good discant, proving that [only] that *discantator* or writer of discants is experienced and wise who knows the natures of the consonances, and how they must be arranged in discant, and which ones are more suitable at the beginning, which in the middle, and which at the end, and in what way they must be varied alternately below and above. Let him consider these and many other things that are required for good discant, and let him observe the final [cause], which is the melodious sound coming forth and rising up from discant, as well as the refreshment of the ears.

Yet some new men, who are perhaps reckoned among the major figures in the composition of discants, are now seen to pursue the formal and final [causes] of discants rather in subtlety of composition, in difficulty, and in intricacy, are seen to be studying [them] here, to take delight there, one against the other. Do not such men change the final [cause], and turn the practice of discants into [theoretical] speculation?

Although some discants may begin, albeit rarely, with imperfect concords such as thirds, like the minor or major third, they must not, however, end with them. Whence, according to Master Franco, there are six consonances with which discants customarily begin: the unison, the octave, the fifth, the fourth, the minor third, and the major third. And he provides examples of [all of] them. But I do not intend to get down into the specific rules of singing discant that may bear on the matter, [or the rules] of the entire sequence of discant, beginning, middle, and end. He who shall wish to attend carefully to the things that have been and shall be said on this matter, and who seeks to acquire greater subtlety in those things, shall perhaps be able, not just to compose plainsongs in any way he chooses and to correct improperly composed ones, but measured ones as well.

<Chapter 6. Whether a fourth beneath a fifth is a consonance.>

It would seem that a fourth beneath a fifth is not a consonance, for the fifth, as a consonance, ranks before the fourth, just as the 3:2 proportion ranks before the 4:3 proportion. Therefore the fourth is a consonance not beneath the fifth, but above [*lit.* before … after].

The opposite position is held by Guido who places the fourth beneath the fifth in the example of discant given before.

Answer. This question has been posed here as one incidental [to our purpose], since Guido, as we have seen, says that there are three consonances that are to be used more principally in discants, namely, the octave, fifth, and fourth as far as the intervals of unequal notes are concerned, and exemplifying this, he places the fourth beneath the fifth. Yet he should not have done this if the fourth were a consonance not beneath the fifth but only above.

Yet a certain modern teacher maintains the opposite in a certain compendious work of the *Musica* of Boethius. And in order that the viewpoint of this teacher be more clearly apparent, let his words be quoted here. Thereafter we shall offer a response to the said question and to the statements of the said teacher. In the eighteenth proposition of the first part of his work, therefore, he says:

> *There is no harmonious agreement whatsoever between the fourth and the octave. The Pythagoreans denied that the octave can be in harmony with the fourth, since it does not enter the hearing either sweetly or smoothly. Investigating the cause of this, they discovered that* [the relation of octave to fourth] *is outside the genus of multiplicity* [$^n/_1$] *and superparticularity* [$^{(n+1)}/_n$], *whereas every perfect consonance is found in those genera.*
>
> Rather it is founded in the double superbipartient proportion [$^{(2n+2)}/_n$], in which 8 relates to 3 [$^{(6+2)}/_3 = 8/_3$ though in this case actually $^{(16+2)}/_8 = 18/_8$], *and they remained silent on this* [proportion] *as though* [it were] *something incongruous. It seems from this that they meant that the raised fourth upon which would be raised a fifth,* that is, a fourth beneath a fifth, *is not a consonance.* Yet it is a consonance when placed above the fifth, *even though in both cases the outer notes span an octave.*
>
> Ptolemy is not in agreement with those men, however, but rather blames them, stating that an octave combined with a fourth is a good consonance; nor, according to him, is it incongruous that it is in the genus of the superbipartiens, because it is in the first species of that genus.
>
> Neither Boethius in his *Musica*, nor the other musicians that I have seen, settle this question. I do know, however, that it is similar to the question whether the fourth beneath a fifth is a consonance, since there is no doubt that it is an excellent consonance above the fifth.
>
> I say, however: If it is granted that the fifth comes before the fourth, just as the 3:2 proportion comes before the 4:3 proportion, then it shall be granted by implication that the fourth beneath a fifth is not a consonance, and neither beneath <or above> the octave, therefore, when the fourth is placed there beneath a fifth. Also, by the nature of consonance, out of which they are made *in the way of numbers and proportions, it is better to make*

them by raising rather than by lowering; therefore the fourth is more consonant above the fifth than beneath it.

Also, the relationship of octave to fifth comes before [its relationship] to the fourth, just as 12 is related to 8 before [it is related] to 9, since 8 precedes 9, and [the fifth precedes] the fourth by one whole tone. It is true inasmuch as the fourth is sound, but not inasmuch it is consonant sound. Also, the whole tone precedes the fourth, yet it is not a consonance, but part of a consonance.

Thus I say that the fourth beneath a fifth is not a consonance, as the Pythagoreans had it, but part of one; above the fifth, however, it must be called a consonance, and thus <the octave> is [a consonance] not of itself but rather out of two consonances, that is, in reality, the fourth and the fifth. When these are placed, it is impossible not to place [the octave as well], except perhaps to the extent that it differs from both. [Muris, *Musica spec.*]

These are the said words of the teacher to which, I think, I would have responded earlier in its proper place, and also to certain other [statements] in the said work, if I had seen it [at that time]. In the words quoted here, the author seems to assert that the question whether the fourth beneath the fifth is a consonance is similar to the question whether the fourth combined with the octave is a good consonance. For he claims to know this. By what proof he knows it I cannot tell, for he does not appear to disclose that [proof]. And having supposed this, he struggles mightily to demonstrate that the fourth beneath the fifth is not a consonance.

However, let us proceed here as follows: First, let us deal with that which this author supposes and claims to know, namely, that the said two questions are similar. Second, let us respond to the principal question, namely, whether the fourth beneath the fifth is a consonance. Third, [let us respond] to the words from the author that have been quoted here.

As to the first, the said two questions do not appear to be similar to one another:

First, because the first question does not seem to be much affected by whether the fourth is placed beneath the octave or above it; this is not true of the second [question], for it is denied that the fourth beneath a fifth is a consonance. That it is a consonance above the fifth, yes, that is conceded, nay more, it is said there to be an excellent consonance.

Second, because the first question is not concerned with whether the fourth differs formally and actually from the octave, but rather with the consonant sound that arises from those two consonances, or that includes those two, given that neither of them is being actively expressed. But this is not the case with the other question, for it supposes that the fourth is actually sung beneath or above the fifth.

Third, because the first question has been well addressed by the authorities of music. For Boethius mentions those [authorities] as well as other teachers in his *Musica*, book 5, chapter 9; and this question has also been addressed above, in the second book of the present work. Yet the second question has not been addressed by any author of music <whose> work I have seen, excepting this one modern author; and I think I have seen fifteen different treatises on music, perhaps even more. And what could be the reason for this unless perhaps some [authors] considered only the first question a [genuine] matter of doubt, but not the second?

Fourth, because with regard to the first question, Ptolemy (and Boethius, who seems to repeat the words of Ptolemy) does not seem to recognize any difference as to whether the fourth is placed beneath or above the octave; this is quite clearly apparent from the examples he gives. But with regard to the second question, this author does recognize a great difference as to whether the fourth is placed beneath or above the fifth.

Fifth, because if there were any similarity between those two questions, then if the fourth is not a consonance beneath the fifth, and yet an excellent consonance above the fifth, then similarly the fourth would be a consonance not beneath the octave, but above the octave. However, this is not what Boethius says, nor Ptolemy, but rather they seem to speak with a certain indifference as to whether the fourth is placed beneath the octave or above it, since its proportion is changed neither here nor there.

From these [arguments], and others that could be brought in as well, it would seem that there is no similarity between those two questions.

<Chapter 7. That the fourth beneath the fifth is a consonance.>

Yet let us now move on to the second question, namely, whether the fourth beneath the fifth is a consonance.

And it must be pointed out that the fourth, when understood in a formal and actual sense, is also a perfect consonance, whether placed by itself, or beneath a fifth, or above; albeit of a lower degree of perfection than some others, as has been seen above in the fourth book. This is what all the ancient musicians whose works I have seen, and modern [musicians] generally as well, appear to maintain unanimously.

If Franco puts the fourth and fifth both among the middle concords, he does so in other that they may be distinguished from the most perfect concords, which are the unison and octave. However, it does not follow: "They are the most perfect concords, therefore they are not perfect ones." For concords may be given [different] degrees, in the sense that some are perfect, some more perfect, and some <most perfect>, as has been seen above. And thus, the ones that we have assigned to the first degree of perfection, for the reasons mentioned above, are classified by Franco among the middle concords. We must look at the thing itself rather than its name.

Now this author, whatever he may say elsewhere in the same work, does seem to hold that the fourth is a perfect consonance. For in the third proposition of that treatise, he says, *that there are now three perfect sounding harmonies*. Those three harmonies, he says, are *the octave in 2:1 proportion, the fifth in 3:2 proportion, and the fourth in 4:3 proportion*. In this way, then, and speaking in an absolute sense, he does call the fourth a perfect harmony.

However, it does not seem that one perfect consonance takes away any perfection from another; all are properly consonant, each as perfect as the other. So if the fourth is a perfect consonance, then an adjoined fifth, which is also perfect whether beneath or above, does not take away its perfection from it. For this is what he says in the exposition of that third proposition: *Experience has taught that there are not fewer than three harmonies, yet whether there are more which nature has wanted to reveal, only God knows. Yet thus far nobody seems to have encountered more perfect ones than these three.*

This statement does not seem to accord with the ancient Pythagorean musicians nor with Ptolemy, who posited other harmonies besides these three, such as the double octave in 4:1 proportion, which Ptolemy calls more perfect than the fourth and fifth because it is equal-sounding, whereas those two are together-sounding. Besides, they classed the fifth plus octave among the consonant harmonies, to which Ptolemy also added the fourth plus octave. Now they did this having been taught by natural reason. Nor was Pythagoras the first to discover those consonances, for music had been discovered a long time before him, and so had been the use of those [consonances], namely before the universal flood.

Therefore I say that the fourth is a true consonance, whether it be taken by itself, or joined beneath a fifth, or above it. This is its intrinsic quality, arising from the good blend of its outermost notes and from the proportion in which it is based.

Therefore I maintain with the ancients that the fourth is a true consonance in itself, different both essentially and specifically from the fifth and the octave, and all the others, just as is the blend of its outermost notes and their specific proportion.

This is the one that Boethius placed among the first consonances. And according to the ancients it is the first and least consonance. The tetrachords are distinguished according to it, and the disposition of the monochord is principally based upon it.

This is the one which the ancients recommend so much, the one that has so many beautiful properties, as seen above. Now, in order for the fourth to be a true consonance, it is not necessary that it be joined to the fifth beneath or above, nor with any other, just as there is no consonance that borrows its nature from another, but rather only from those things of which we have said above, in the second book, that they are necessary for consonant sound; and all are distinguished from one another by species or genus.

The nature of any consonance, therefore, is maintained when it is placed by itself, and more so, it seems, than when it is joined to some other one in one fashion or another. For when it is taken by itself, the more the blend of its notes is apparent, so that it is distinguished from others. And this blend does not change, no matter what other consonances it may be joined to, just as its proportion is neither. For it that were the case, then that consonance would be subject to corruption.

None of this diminishes the fact that some consonances sound better in one place than another, or better with others than by themselves, for reasons already mentioned or yet to be mentioned.

<Chapter 8. Why the notes of the fourth make better concord above the fifth than beneath it.>

It has been sufficiently noted that the fourth, as manifested in actuality, is of better concordant sound above the fifth than beneath it. For the sense judges this to be so. However, there must be some reason for this difference, for according to Plato, in the first book of *Timaeus*, *there is nothing whose birth has not been preceded by a lawful cause.*

If I knew what [that reason] was, I would gladly state it. Some would say (and the said teacher appears to be among their number), that the reason for this is that the fifth is a prior and more perfect consonance than the fourth. And this argument is confirmed, for when two consonances immediately follow one another, then it would be more appropriate for the greater and more perfect one to be beneath the lesser and more imperfect one, and to support it, rather than the other way round. It must be pointed out that if this is indeed more appropriate, it does not mean that we now have a reason that sufficiently [answers] the said question, for according to the said reason, as already mentioned, the fourth would sound better above the octave than beneath. And that is not granted.

Others have perhaps proposed other reasons for the said difference. I shall mention, without prejudice of any kind, the one that I consider the more true.

I say, therefore, that if the notes of the fourth are more greatly concordant above the fifth than beneath it, then this seems to be the case because its high note is supported in that place, since it coincides with the high note of the octave, and its low note with the high note of the fifth, and thus it seems to be reinforced there. And in this way the concord of the fourth is increased by two that are better [concords] than itself. Yet this is not the case when it is placed beneath the fifth. For in that position, its two notes are supported by, or coincide with, the lower notes of the said consonances.

For concordant sound is produced by higher notes more than by lower ones, and experience as well as sense teaches that this is so. This is borne out by the fact that the high note seems to be more perfect than the low one, because the low one is closer to silence than the high one, just as sluggish and slow movement is closer to the state of rest than fast. And when one man goes up from low notes to high ones, he seems to be breathing out more air on the high ones than onthe low ones, and also to make more and more forceful movements.

The process of heightening the pitch, which is a certain quality, seems to be similar to the heightening of some other quality, say, of color or whiteness. For there, too, there is a process moving from the lesser degree of such a form to a greater and more perfect one.

From this it seems that the discantus should keep itself above the tenor rather than the other way round, for high notes that bring in the concordant sound of consonances are more suitable for the discantus, and low ones for the tenor.

What seems to produce the said effect, as mentioned already, is that two causes work together when something is attached to them: one is that the more perfect and greater consonance is beneath the lesser and more imperfect one; the other, that the extreme boundaries of those two consonances make a perfect and simple proportion by themselves. Now when the fourth is beneath the fifth, then the first of those causes is eliminated; and when the fourth is placed above the octave, then the second [is eliminated]. These reasons are in great agreement: the first pertains to concordant notes, the second to proportions.

From these things, if they are true, we can explain why the fourth is of better concordant sound above the fifth than above the octave, for when it is placed above the octave in actual fact, then its high note is supported by nothing except itself alone. [This modern teacher,] having made the comparison of that high note to the low note of the octave, arrives at the duple superbipartient proportion in which good concords do not seem to be based, as the Pythagoreans maintained.

Yet it is apparent from what we have said that in order to increase the concord of some consonance, it is more effective to have its high note coincide with the high note of a better consonance, than have the low note of the fourth coincide with the high note of the octave. For [in that case] its concord seems to be increased but little.

Now we can tell, from what we have said, why the fourth makes more concord above a fifth which is placed upon an octave, than directly upon the octave itself, for in that place the high note of the fourth coincides with the high note of the double octave. Hence the fourth makes excellent concord in two places, namely, where its high note coincides with the high note of the octave and [where it coincides with the high note] of the double octave.

And if the imperfect concord is made perfect before a perfect one, because of the way it leans upon it, it seems reasonable that some concord, say, of the fourth, must be increased by the more perfect one if it communes with it.

It is now apparent, from what we have said, that since the fourth makes more concord above the fifth than beneath it, the octave is more effective in this regard than the fifth. From all this we can recognize the good concord of the fifth, whose outermost notes make concord together well, no matter where they are placed. Unlike the fourth, there is no need for its high note to coincide with the high note of the octave in order for its concord to be increased. For in that case it would sound better if it were placed in the high part of the octave rather than the low part.

From what we have said, we can now recognize the excellent concord of the octave and double octave relative to the fifth, for the concord of the fourth is not amplified nearly so much when its high note coincides with the high note of the fifth, than when it coincides with the high note of the octave or double octave.

Yet let this incidental digression now be at an end. Let us return to the subject.

<Chapter 9. Of foolish discantors.>

If discant, as we have already seen, must be made from not just any interval, then how can those individuals who have learned little or nothing about the nature of consonances, who are unable to tell which ones are more concordant or less, which are not, and which are to be used more often and in what places, and who do not know the other things that are necessary to this art, [how can they] have the temerity to sing and make discant?

Do not such men sing discant arbitrarily? Do not such men pronounce their notes over a tenor uncertain [to them]? If they could make concord at all, they would make it, for what it is worth, like a pebble that is thrown at an uncertain target, that would [only accidentally] strike or hit the target, if indeed it could strike or hit it at all.

Some of those ignorant men are not afraid even to sing discant in God's Holy Church Militant, where there ought to be neither wrinkle nor stain. Whence it comes that they often bring the stain of discord into [the church]. Such men bring disorder to discant, they sometimes mutilate, diminish, and corrupt the concords with respect to their [underlying] rationale. And if, once in a while, they happen to make a concord with the tenor, they are unable to remain in concord because of their ignorance of the said art, and thus quickly fall back into discord.

Alas! Some people nowadays attempt to gild over their defects with the help of a foolish saying. "This," they say, "is the new way of singing discant," that is, of using new consonances. These men offend the intellect of those who are able to recognize such defects. They offend the sense, for when they should be bringing delight, they bring sadness.

Oh, what wayward saying! Oh, what wicked gilding-over, what irrational excuse! Oh, what great abuse, what great brutishness, what great beastliness, when an ass is taken for a human, a she-goat for a lion, a sheep for a fish, a serpent for a salmon! For the concords are so different from the discords that one is in no way like the other.

Oh, if the ancient experienced teachers of music had heard such discantors, what would they have said, what would they have done? They would rebuke the one singing discant, saying: "Do not sing the kind of discant you're using [with what I sing]. Do not [try to] make one song, that is, a concordant one, with me. What are you doing here? You are disagreeable to me, inimical to me, offensive to me. How I wish you could stay silent. You do not make concord, you are raving and making discord."

There are also those who take it upon themselves to sing discant but are not able to sing well or [to sing] steadily, even though discant is a certain kind of song and measurable song presupposes the plain chant.

There are also some who do not observe the good manner, although they have learned a little to sing discant. They sing discant too frivolously, they multiply superfluous notes. Some of them apply hocket too much, they break consonant notes too often, run up and divide up, they leap in unsuitable places, they clash, they bellow, and they yelp and bark after the manner of dogs, and like insane people, they take nourishment from a disorganized and convoluted ruckus, they use a harmony that is far removed from nature.

For according to Guido harmonious sound is threefold: a certain kind is far removed from nature, as when somebody sings chant or discant too frivolously, singing organum with subtlety of the windpipes, and multiplies notes with superfluity; another natural one which is ruled by moderateness of harmony, and this is the authentic one in God's Church, because it is simple and modest; and the third is most plain, when the chant relates to the organum, or the other way round, that is, when the tenor makes concord with the discantus.

Nowadays there are also many good and capable musicians, singers, and discantors, who know how to sing discant not just from practical use but from art, and who make many beautiful discants. Yet they use the new manner of singing and abandon the old one; they use imperfect [concords] much, they take pleasure in those semibreves that they call minims, they cast away from them the old organal songs, the conducti, the *motelli*, the hockets, double, contradouble, and triple, unless they can graft some of [that music] into their own motets or *motelli*. They put together discants that are subtle and difficult to sing and to measure. And just as they distance themselves, in their manner of singing, from ancients [such as] Franco, Aristoteles, and others, so do they in their manner of notating measured songs, as shall be discussed below.

Having considered these things, let us now speak of the species of discant, which are many.

<Chapter 10. The distinction between discants.>

Diaphonia or *discantus* is distinguished in many ways. According to one way, [they can be distinguished] according to the consonances from which they are made, as when someone who, while singing discant, uses fifths more amply, more frequently, and as it were [commanded] by the Lord, is said to *diapentizare* or *quinthiare*, or, when he uses fourths more amply, to *quartare* or *diatesseronare*, and likewise with the others.

With regard to the manner of singing, however, discants vary in many ways. For there is a certain discant in simple fashion which is measured in every of its parts by certain tempus. Another is the discant fashioned in that *organum duplum which is called organum proprie dictum* [properly so-called] or *purum. Commonly*, as Franco says, *any ecclesiastical song which is measured in tempora is called organum.*

Discant in a simple sense is divided into truncated discant, which is called *hoketus*, coupled discant, which is called *copula* or fast discant, discant performed in simple fashion, and this manner of singing discant is found in ecclesiastical or organal discants that are measured in all their parts, in conducti, in *motelli*, in *fugi*, and in *cantilenae* or *rondelli*.

Also, there are [types] of discant that have the same text or different ones: the same [text] in *cantilenae* and in some ecclesiastical chants, different [texts] in motets that have a triplum. Discant with and without text is found in conducti and in a certain kind of song that is improperly called organum.

Also, according to the moderns, discants can be distinguished according to tempus and measure, for some are called "of perfect tempus," others "of imperfect tempus," which are now much in use. They however call songs "regular" when perfect is sung against perfect, and imperfect against imperfect. There are other discants in which imperfect is sung against perfect, and the other way round, and these they call "irregular."

Now, according to the moderns, just like it would be to present perfect notes perfectly, imperfect ones perfectly, perfect ones imperfectly, imperfect ones imperfectly, so, accordingly, shall it be to present perfect discants perfectly, imperfect ones perfectly, perfect ones imperfectly, and imperfect ones imperfectly.

Also, according to the moderns, there are certain discants that are in perfect modus and tempus, others in imperfect modus and tempus, other in perfect modus but not tempus, others the other way round, and yet others partly perfect and partly imperfect, in modus as well as tempus.

Now, to what avail are such and similar intrications and subtiliations if not [theoretical] speculation?

They posit many other distinctions between discants, about which [we will say] nothing at present, for in these things they seem to subvert the principal aim of those discants. For they lead the art, which is truly and principally a practical one, away into subtlety and speculation, and thus they confuse practice and speculation. But what is the use of subtlety when usefulness is lost? If only they would study the noble *musica* that is truly speculative, there they could find their foundation, there they could acquire more subtlety, and would not draw practical music outside of its boundaries.

Since we have spoken of discant (and discant pertains to measurable music), we must now look into measure and tempus, and thence onward into the notes or figures by which measurable songs are notated, and the values and properties.

<Chapter 11. What is tempus as it pertains to measurable music.>

Tempus taken in the general sense, or so a certain modern teacher says, *is the measure of sound produced in one continuous movement*. Interrupted movement, on the other hand, is not continuous. This seems to be the case with the movement measuring *tempus longum*. For this teacher says that *tempus longum is that which is divided into three parts, and parts of parts, down to the shortest sound*. He does not say that it is "divisible," but [rather that it] "is divided." But that which is in actual fact separated into three parts, or more or fewer, is not continuous, and accordingly, this definition of tempus does not seem to have general validity, since it does not apply to *tempus longum*. Below it shall be noted that measurable music pertains not just to tempus that is continuous, but also [that which is] discrete, and perhaps even more so.

Master Franco describes tempus as follows: *Tempus is the measure both of sound that is uttered and of its opposite, that is, sound muted which is called a rest. For if a rest is not measured by tempus, then two tunes, of which one has rests and the other does not, could not be related to each other on a basis of equality*.

Another teacher, who is named Aristoteles, speaks thus: *Tempus, as understood here, is the just proportion in which the recta <brevis has a figure in such*

a proportion that it can be divided only into two parts that are unqueal, or in three that are equal and> indivisible, in such a way that the sound cannot be further divided in time.

Although this description is given specifically for [the quantity of] time carried by a *recta* or perfect brevis, it may be extended also to the [quantities of] time represented by other notes. By "just proportion" he understands here a certain interval or measure of time which he specifies when he says "in which the *recta brevis*..." and so on. He says "*recta brevis*" to distinguish it from the *brevis altera* which corresponds to two *rectae breves*. And to that extent the [*brevis altera*] is identical to the imperfect longa, in that both [this note] and the other carry two imperfect tempora. Also, by speaking [only] of *recta* or perfect *brevis*, he excludes the imperfect breve posited by the moderns.

The said description of tempus is opposed in several ways by some of the moderns, as shall become apparent in what follows.

<Chapter 12. How the previously stated description of tempus is being attacked by the moderns.>

Let us however consider in what way the moderns oppose the description of perfect tempus given earlier

Perfect tempus as understood by the ancients, they say, is a certain equal proportion in which the *recta brevis* is divided either into two unequal parts or into three equal ones, which can never in turn be divided or distinguished further. This description of perfect tempus, which is from the teacher who is called Aristoteles, as said above, is attacked by the moderns for being, first, insufficient, and second, at variance with the truth. It is insufficient, they say, because just as perfect tempus is divisible into two unequal parts or in three equal ones, so, in the same way, is it divisible into two equal parts, with the value of tempus nevertheless remaining the same. The said description of tempus does not however mention this [alternative division]. Therefore, [they conclude,] it must be judged insufficient.

The moderns also say that it is not true that the three equal parts into which perfect tempus is divided are [themselves] indivisible, since any one of them may be divisible in three in modern practice. They demonstrate the first [argument], among others, as follows: a continuous body, before it will be divided in actual fact, is [potentially] divisible into two equal parts, just as it is in three, or into two unequal parts. Therefore the same shall be true of tempus, since it is a species of continuous quantity. And they demonstrate the second [argument] as follows: first, because of the different figuration of semibreves, which [figuration] would not be needed if they were confined to so small a number; second, because it would not be possible otherwise to notate more than nine semibreves in the place of a perfect longa of three tempora; third, because imperfect tempus is divisible <in more parts> than three and hence tempus perfectum, which it is the more preeminent and more important, even more so; fourth, because the third part of perfect tempus could then be made equal to a *recta brevis*; fifth, because the tongue and throat, and other natural instruments, are able to produce more than three. Therefore, and so on.

Let us proceed in defense of the description of perfect tempus given before, in this way: first, we shall respond to the said first [argument], in which it is attacked for being insufficient; secondly, to the second. As far as the first [point] is concerned, first it shall be demonstrated that it is repugnant for perfect tempus to be divisible into two equal parts; second, this shall be affirmed in order that the ancients, against whom the moderns are speaking, should be the more vindicated.

<Chapter 13. That it is repugnant for perfect tempus to be divisible into two equal parts.>

For the [reasons] to be stated [below], it seems repugnant for perfect tempus, as distinguished from imperfect, to be divisible into two equal parts.

Firstly, this is proved by the statements of those men, for the division of tempus that they have made – which is that one is perfect, the other imperfect – is in itself repugnant. For the members of this division, if what they say here is true, are actually the same thing [i.e indistinguishable], and this is what I have promised above I would demonstrate.

For if it is appropriate for perfect tempus, being one member of the division and thus distinct from imperfect tempus, to be divided into two equal parts (which is appropriate to imperfect tempus, as is indeed stated, according to them, in his description), and if similarly it would be appropriate, as they assert, for imperfect tempus to be divided into three parts, then what is the consequence of this, if not that perfect tempus is imperfect, and vice versa? For things are the same when their definitions are the same.

Yet since the moderns have [already] in some way foreseen this objection, they who are expounding [their teachings] labor hard to answer it. And they say that, strictly speaking, it is not called imperfect tempus because it is divisible or divided into two equal parts. For in that case perfect tempus could also truthfully be called imperfect, namely when it is divided equally into two parts. Nor is <perfect> tempus so called because it is divisible into three equal parts, for then imperfect [tempus] could also be called perfect. Rather, it it is called imperfect because it does not attain the perfect value of perfect tempus, but contains only two parts of it [i.e., the imperfect breve is two-thirds of a perfect breve, no matter how it will be divided]

This answer has no merit, however, for they who say this make a distinction between perfect and imperfect tempus with regard to matter, but not with regard to form. And matter cannot be a criterion of distinction, since according to Averroes, there are no distinctions in the very foundation of nature, that is, in [prime] matter. It is the actual deed [of formation] which distinguishes and separates, as stated in <the sixth book > of *Metaphysics*.

What I seek to know from them, then, is the *formal* rationale by which perfect tempus is distinguished from imperfect. Therefore, etc.

Third, this same point is borne out as follows, namely, that it is inherent in perfection that something contains three equal parts into which it is divisible, and that it is reducible, it seems, to the ratio of the ternary number, to which it is completely repugnant to contain two equal parts in which it be divisible, [parts] which would add up to it precisely if they were joined together. And for the same reason it is repugnant to imperfect tempus, as specifically distinct from perfect, to contain three equal parts – just as [repugnant] as it is to the binary number, because of its imperfection, when [such division] is applied.

Also, as will be seen below, measurable music does not pertain just to continuous tempus, on which the modern teachers rely too much, but also to tempus as counted and differentiated.

<Chapter 14. Confirmation of the things said.>

In order to confirm the things said, and to offer a stronger defense of the ancients, let us here expand on the reason or reasons wherefore perfect tempus is said to be divisible into three equal parts, and wherefore it is repugnant to it to be split into two equal parts, and, for another part, wherefore it is rational to call that tempus imperfect to which it is appropriate to contain within itself two equal parts, not three, because of the rationale proper to it, as distinguished from perfect.

These things are appropriate to them, it seems, on account of their name "perfect," in order to uphold its name since it is called "perfect," and similarly [in the case of] "imperfect." For according to Aristotle, in the first book of *On the Heavens*, and also according to the Pythagoreans (as he says in the same place), we use this predicate, that is, "all," in the first instance for [things that come] in threes [rather than twos]. Which is to say that in the first place one speaks only of "all" about threes. And according to the same Aristotle in his *Metaphysics*, *all things that are whole and perfect are the same.*

Accordingly, therefore, we call that tempus perfect which takes its name from the ternary number, and [we call] that imperfect which [takes its name] from the binary. For the binary number, as seen above, is called ill-famed and imperfect, not only because it is the first to depart from unity [the number one], but also because it contains within itself two parts, [and thus] that it is completely repugnant to it to contain three. But the first thing called perfect is that [which comes] in threes. [Accordingly] that which is imperfect is relative to the perfect.

Grant, therefore, that if perfect would be divisible into two equal parts, it would be imperfect. In that case it is necessary for it to be relative to something [else that is] perfect. And about that [perfect thing], I ask if it is divisible into two equal parts or not. For if it is, then it, too, shall be imperfect, and [hence] relative to something else that is perfect, just as in the previous case. And in this way there shall be infinite regress. It would have been better to insist from the beginning that it is repugnant to perfect tempus, as formally distinguished from imperfect, to be divisible into two equal parts, which [divisibility] is the rationale of imperfect tempus.

To this extent ternareity designates perfection, since, according to Aristotle in the first book of *On the Heavens*, only corporeal quantity should be called perfect, as it includes within itself three dimensions: length, width, and depth; not so line, or area. Also God, who is most perfect in himself and from whom proceeds all perfection, so much commends for perfection to consist in the ternary number, that in him, the most perfect threeness is [coextensive] with the most singular oneness. And threeness may inhere also in all other things to some extent, since every created thing was made either after the likeness of God, like Angels and humans, or after God's imprint, like other creatures. For *he has made all things in number, weight, and measure* [Wisdom 11: 21]. God rejoices in odd number. Among the Angels there are three hierarchies, each of which is in turn divided by the ternary number.

Aristotle, too, has posited the first principles of three things.

Also, all rectilinear shapes are reducible to the triangle, which is the first rectilinear shape. Hence, when the triangle is reduced, it is reduced in three triangles, the quadrangle into four triangles, the pentagon into five, the hexagon into six, and so forth, as can be seen in the second book of Boethius's *Arithmetic*. And Jordanus of Nemore holds the same in his *Arithmetic*. For two lines do not make a shape, but rather an opening. For a shape must be completely closed, since a shape is that which is closed in a boundary or boundaries, as Boethius says. (He speaks of [one] "boundary" on account of circular shape, and of "boundaries" on account of rectilinear [shapes], which have angles.)

We could cite many other authors and various examples [to show] that threeness <is synonymous> with perfection. Both the ancients and the moderns are concur with those opinions.

Now, although it is repugnant for perfect tempus to be split up into two equal parts, it is appropriate for it to be split into two unequal parts, and in this regard it is comparable to a perfect church mode which is divisible into two unequal parts, but not into two equal parts, like the imperfect tone, which this regard is comparable on this point to imperfect tempus.

<Chapter 15. That division into whole parts is repugnant to the semibreve.>

Having refuted the opinion of those who say that the perfect breve is partible into two equal parts, let us move on to what they say about the division of semibreves.

When the ancients, they say, call the semibreves indivisible, then this is not true according to the moderns, since any one of the three semibreves into which the perfect breve is said to be divisible would in turn be divisible into three [notes] that are called minims.

Let us deal first with this statement; secondly, let us respond to certain arguments that are adduced by the moderns; thirdly, let us defend the ancients and explain why they held that semibreves are indivisible.

As to the first, we argue as follows. The division which marks the last and final division of the musical notes of the measurable art is repugnant to those notes, that is, to the semibreve inasmuch as it is a semibreve. Therefore, and so forth. For the major semibreve this is self-evident, but let us demonstrate it for the minor. It seems, then, that division of the integral whole is repugnant to the semibreve. And its form denotes its indivisibility in some way. For [the semibreve] is shaped in the manner of a lozenge, which has a point at the top, and ends in a point at the bottom. Now division of continuous quantity, of which we are speaking here, stops at the point, since this [is and] remains completely indivisible through quantitative division. Thus Euclid, in the first book of his *Geometry*: *A point is that of which there is no part*. And Aristotle in the third book of *On the soul*: *A point*, he says, *and all indivisibility*, [is known by privation]. Yet this is not the case with the shapes of the long and breve.

But perhaps [this] shall be opposed for the major semibreve, which according to the ancients [also] has the form and name of a semibreve. For this [major semibreve] does appear to be divisible, since it contains within itself two parts of the perfect breve, that is, two [of those] semibreves of which three make up the perfect breve.

Now it must be said, first of all, that the said case does not apply as far as the moderns are concerned, not only because they class [this value] among the breves rather than semibreves, but also because they hold that the semibreve which carries the third part of the perfect breve, or half of the imperfect, is divisible.

Second, it must be said that if division were appropriate to a semibreve of this kind, then it is appropriate not inasmuch as it is a semibreve, but rather inasmuch as such a semibreve contains within itself two parts of the perfect breve, because in this regard it does share the principle of the whole [breve]. But this is a division into parts that have the same form and name [as the whole], in the manner of a whole that is homogeneous [lit. of one kind]. But we are not principally speaking of this [sort of] whole, but rather of a whole that is heterogeneous [lit. of neither kind].

Third, it must be said that this division, or rather accepting, of two minor semibreves for a major semibreve is to be construed, not as a division of the major semibreve, but rather of the breve. For according to the ancients, the minor semibreve does not relate to the major semibreve as a part [does] to the whole, but rather they relate to each other as two distinct species [of the same thing], like when it is said that some semibreves are major, and others minor.

Now one species is not a part of another [species]. The same can be said of the *altera brevis* as distinct from the perfect breve, namely, that it is not appropriate for it to be divided into two perfect breves, since [a single breve] does not relate to [the *altera brevis*] as a part to the whole. Also, if it is in the nature of the semibreve, which is the third part of the perfect breve, that it be divisible in three, then that semibreve will be divisible no matter how quickly the perfect breve were to be performed. But this is not apparent. Therefore it is not appropriate for it to be divided inasmuch as it is a semibreve (and that is what it is), but rather as [a note that] is performed slowly.

<Chapter 16. Response to the counter-arguments.>

Yet let us now respond to some of the arguments of those who posit that the semibreve is divisible. It is possible to offer one general response, mentioned earlier, to those [arguments]. If division be appropriate to an interval of time carrying the semibreve, this can be understood in two ways. One way, that such an interval of time is taken in a material and absolute sense, like some continuous quantity, and that it is in this sense appropriate for it to be divided. Another way, that [the interval] is signified by the semibreve, and in this sense the division of which we are speaking is repugnant to it. So it does not follow: Such an interval of time is divisible, therefore the semibreve is divisible.

But let us respond specifically to the things that are said on the opposite side. They say: *semibreves are figured in different ways; this would not be necessary unless they were divisible* (one must say: *they are by destruction*). Conclusion: *they are figurable in different ways; therefore they are divisible.* Now it is one thing to be figured, but another to be divided. And in the proof of that conclusion it seems that the fallacy of "consequence from insufficiency" [i.e., from too few premises] is committed, for [semibreves] may be figured in this way or that for a different reason than the indication of their division. Also, the ancients rejected the antecedent, that is, that semibreves taken by themselves are figurable in different ways (and the reason for this will be stated below).

Secondly they say: *If semibreves were not to be divisible, then it would not be possible to notate more than nine semibreves for the perfect longa of three tempora.* It must be pointed out that this does not follow, least of all when such a longa is measured slowly. For it could be measured so fast that it would scarcely be possible to notate even nine semibreves for it, as the ancients sometimes did. Nor, for that matter, is division of semibreves to be deduced from the notation of three semibreves for a perfect breve, but rather only immediate [division] of breves, or mediate [division] of longas. For when one semibreve be distinguished from another by species or number, it is not one part or the whole of the other.

Thirdly they say: *Imperfect tempus is divisible in more than three; therefore tempus perfectum even more so.* It must be pointed out that those who argue thus, having granted the antecedent and granted the conclusion, do not have a point, for the division of semibreves is not to be deduced from the notation of more than three semibreves for perfect or imperfect tempus, but rather [the division] of breves, unless the interval of time carried by the semibreve were understood in a material sense. Also, the ancients rejected the antecedent, and they did not notate that imperfect breve which the moderns notate.

They add, fourthly: *If the semibreve were not divisible, then the third part of the perfect breve would be equated to a breve.* It must be said that this is possible for tempus taken in a material sense, for something can only occupy so much from the tempus in the performance of one semibreve as another in the performance of a perfect breve. It does not follow from this that the breve is a semibreve or the other way round. It does not follow either that the semibreve is divisible.

Nor is there validity to what they say, fifthly: *The throat with other instruments producing sound can produce more than three [sounds] for the recta brevis; therefore the semibreve is divisible.* This does not follow; what does follow is that the *recta brevis* is divisible in more than three semibreves, or that more than three semibreves can be taken for the breve. Whence the position that if more semibreves than three, or than four, five, six, seven or eight can be notated for perfect tempus, that the semibrevis <is> indivisible, for this conclusion is contained in the antecedent.

<Chapter 17. Defense of the ancients, and exposition of the things they said, as it touches upon the matter at hand.>

For a better defense of the ancients and a [better] understanding of the things they said, it must be noted that the mensuration of musical notes (longs, breve, and semibreve) is twofold or threefold, namely, fast, slow, and moderate. And the moderns bear witness to this.

For one of them says: *Our singing is threefold, either drawn-out, or fast, or moderate, and in whatever way it may be done, the manner of notating is not to be changed.* And another, ascribing this to perfect tempus, speaks thus: *One should know that perfect tempus is threefold: least, middle, and greatest.*

It must be said, therefore, that where the ancients have said that perfect tempus is not divisible into more than three semibreves, they understand this about the fast mensuration, and a certain modern teacher confirms this about Franco.

For he says that Franco posited the least tempus when the breve is divided into three semibreves that are so tight that they are not divisible any further. And it is evident that Franco understands thusly. For, when he had said that one cannot accept more than three of the semibreves, he at once places himself under: *for this reason*, he say, *that such a semibreve of which I speak is the smallest part of the breve.* And one cannot give smaller than the smallest, not is the smallest divisible.

In that place, then, Franco understands by semibreve, which is the third part of the perfect breve, the very same thing as what the moderns understand by the *minima* or *athoma* when they notate the <ninth> part of perfect tempus, and all indivisibly.

From these things it is apparent that Franco has already posited those smallest semibreves [*minimae*] which the moderns boast having invented. For one speaks thus: *To confess the truth, no other magister than sound reason has taught me about the smallest semibreves.*

Also, when the ancients said that the perfect breve is divisible into three semibreves and not in more, they had in mind that which happened more generally and more regularly, especially in motets. Which is that they notated two unequal or three equal semibreves for a perfect tempus, and not more.

I have said "in motets," for if we speak about *duplex* or *contraduplex* hockets and certain other measured songs, the perfect breve has such a fast measure, according to the ancients, that three semibreves cannot be uttered well or easily for it. Thence, as for the longs and breves with which such songs were notated, it does not seem that was has a place here is a fast mensaration, but rather the fastest possible, so the the perfect breve is held here no longer than the smallest semibreve is now.

But the moderns now use the slow measure very much. And among the moderns the third part of a perfect breve is now worth just as much as the perfect breve itself among the ancients, for it is measured so slowly that it, and as much perfect breve as the perfect long among the old. Thence it is that they would ascribe to the semibreve, which is the third part of the perfect breve, what is breve, that is, that it is divisible, and many other things which are not appropriate to this according to those who had imposed its meaning on it in the beginning.

So although the ancients had generally used a fast mensuration of breves in motets or the fastest possible in *duplex* hockets, once in a while however they went beyond that to the slow and moderate, albeit rarely, in which they notated more than three semibreves for perfect tempus. For that worthy singer, Petrus de Cruce, who composed so many beautiful and good measurable songs, and who followed the art of Franco, sometimes notated more than three semibreves for the perfect breve.

For it was he who began to notate four semibreves for perfect tempus in that triplum:

immediately thereupon:

and elsewhere in that same [triplum] he notated four semibreves for one perfect tempus. Thereafter he went even further and notated, for one perfect tempus, sometimes five semibreves, sometimes six, sometimes seven, in that triplum:

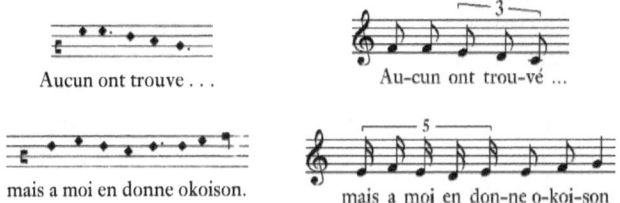

First here are notated five semibreves for one perfect tempus. Thereafter follows two unequal semibreves for the same tempus. Then an imperfect long of two perfect tempora. Also, in that same [triplum], he notated six here:

Thereafter seven here:

li ai fait houmage pour

But another [time] he notated for perfect tempus not just five, six, and seven semibreves, but even eight and on occasion nine, as can be seen in the triplum which begins as follows:

Mout ont chante d'amours, et cetera.

And in the same [triplum] in two place nine [semibreves] are notated for one tempus, but eight are notated only in place, namely, here:

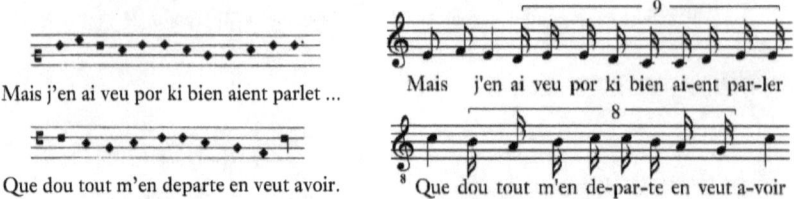
Mais j'en ai veu por ki bien aient parlet ...
Que dou tout m'en departe en veut avoir.

Also, it seems to me that at Paris a triplum has [been] heard that was composed by magister Franco, as people said, in which more than three semibreves were notated for one perfect tempus. And those worthy teachers of music, and others of that same time, have never stated that semibreves are divisible, caudatable, or occurring singly; they have never assigned to them the property that [semibreves] occurring singly could imperfect longs notated by themselves, and breves, and one another. But we will speak of these things below. Those teachers perfectly distinguished those [notes] from each other, whether for one perfect tempus one notated two unequal semibreves, or three equal ones, four, five, six, seven, eight, or nine.

Now, however, in distinguishing their semibreves, the moderns are laboring much in their treatises, but they are not agreeing well. For how many varieties have they used in [their treatises]? And who could say from what they have begun this new manner of singing?

Now it is to be noted that the moderns never seem to notate four semibreves, nor five, nor seven, nor eight for perfect or imperfect tempus, but only two, three, six, or nine. And since the moderns proclaim the nine which they notate for perfect tempus, or the six for imperfect, to be ternary [numbers], and would thus distinguish those which they call minims, it does not seem that those nine are for one perfect tempus but rather for three, so that one perfect tempus would correspond by threes and threes, just as was the case among the ancients. And the latter, indeed, when they notated six or nine for perfect tempus, they thus proclaimed those equally so that they would not distinguish ternaries, binaries, or quaternaries. And since the ancients would notate sometimes four, sometimes five, seven, or eight, for perfect tempus, one could ask the modern they would reduce those to a division of what semibreves; and since they do not invent this, it is necessary that they be reduced to a division of the breve.

Now, from the things [we have] said, it is apparent that the ancients notated and performed, for the same interval of time, two unequal semibreves against three equal ones, against four, five, six, seven, eight, nine. The modern never seem to do this.

Yet so far this has been considered about measure and tempus. Let us consider hereafter about notes or figures of measured songs. First, however, let us say something about the modes, following the order of Franco. We shall see, then, what is modus, and how many modi there are.

<Chapter 18. What is modus.>

Modus, according to Franco, *is the knowledge of sound measured in long and short tempora*. Here, he understands by "sound" some song as a whole that is measured and put together from longs, breves, and semibreves. And thus the modi are distinguished through one or other disposition of longs, breves, and semibreves.

Therefore Aristoteles holds that mode consists of the singing and disposition of sounds. For *mode or manner as understood here*, he says, *is whatever is sung through the proper temporal measure of long and short figures and semibreves*. And what he understand by "temporal measure" has been explained above.

In another way, modus is described thus: *Mode is the arrangement of figures representing diverse affections of the soul in songs* (perhaps because some [belong] more to one mode than to another).

Also, in yet another way: *Mode is a manner of singing which is put together from longs, or long perfections, on the basis of equivalence*. And according to that description, mode does not seem to apply to songs put together from imperfect things, as nevertheless attested by one modern teacher who uses imperfects.

What then is mode in measurable music if not the appropriate order, disposition, or joining together of figures or musical notes, that is, of longs, breves, and semibreves, with respect to each other? That is why the modes vary amongst themselves according to the varying disposition of the said notes, just as, in plain music, the church modes or tones vary in songs because of the varying disposition of sounds at the beginning, middle, and end. (Though this and the other case are not totally comparable.)

<Chapter 19. How many modes there are.>

Certain [writers] have posited nine modes in mensural music, others seven, others six, others five like magister Franco, *because*, as he says, *the others are reducible to five.*

Now the first mode, according to Franco, consists wholly of perfect longs and, under this first mode, he also places the one which consists of an imperfect long and a perfect breve, since they have similar rests. (Some, however, make two modes from this mode.)

The second proceeds by a breve and long.
The third by a long and two breves.
The fourth the other way round.
The fifth by breves and semibreves.

The fact that these are sufficient may be understood thus. It has been said that mode consists of the order and the joining together of the said notes between them. Therefore, either a long is immediately joined together with a long; or a long with a breve, or with breves; or breves between them, without longs, and [also] with their equivalent, that is, with semibreves.

In the first way, thus is the first mode which principally consists wholly of longs or [in which] the long is joined immediately with a breve; and this is twofold, for the single long is accompanied either by a single breve or by several breves. If in the first way, then either the long comes before [the breve] and then that makes the first mode; or the breve [comes before] the long, and that makes the second mode. But if the long is joined with several breves, that is, with two or three, then either the long precedes those breves, and that makes the third mode, or the other way round, and that makes the fourth. Or the breve is arranged with a breve or its equivalent, without longas, and that makes the fifth mode.

So far the order of the said modes seems rational: the first comes before the second like the long [comes] before the breve; the first and second before the third and fourth, because the relationship of longs to long or to a breve is prior that of breves; also, four come before the fifth as a long [comes before] before the breve and semibreve. Others distinguish them however in a different way, while agreeing on the number and order of the said modes.

Thus the first is said to consist wholly of perfect [numbers three], or of the binary number preceding, and the number one [*unitas*] following. The second [is said to consist] of the number one preceding, and the binary number following. The third [is said to consist] of the perfect [number three] preceding, and the number one following twice, of which numbers the last represents the meaning of the binary number. The fourth is made the other way round. The fifth [is said to consist] only of the number one, as well as fractions of the same. This author understands by the binary number the imperfect long, by the number one the breve, by fractions semibreves. Thus he calls the notes by their natural names.

Yet there are some who make two modes from the first mode, and so they posit six modes. And in arranging these, they place the one which is [arranged] wholly of longs in the fifth order, which is more appropriately placed in the first, as the perfect long is the root and foundation of all other modes, and all others flow from perfect longs, and go back to [the perfect long] on the basis of a certain equivalence. Affirming this, Aristoteles speaks thusly:

The first mode is called
The one that is put together only
From perfect figures,
As is shown by the following
Song which is assembled
Out of pure perfects, as here:

[Example supplied after the treatise of Lambertus.]

It appears from this, therefore,
That never pressed together
Into ligatures is this [mode]
But [being] *free it is left out*
And [being] *alone it does not suffer,*
Ever, from things that will oppress.
It rules and is not ruled;
It commands and does not depend
On the cares of others.

From this it is apparent that this teacher denies that the perfect long is ligatable, and that any [long] whatsoever must be notated by itself. And if the *simplex* long is not immediately ligatable to every similar long, then all the less ligatable is the *duplex* or *triplex* long, whether [it be] perfect or imperfect.

Now one should that singers do not exclusively apply the said modes in such a way that one whole song would always go according to one mode, but sometimes one mode is varied into another.

Yet the moderns do not use all the said modes as the ancients did. Also, in all modes, as far as the ancient songs are concerned, the perfection begin together and end together; but not so in modern songs. Also, the ancients used perfects just like this in all their modes and songs, and the perfect measure as well. But not so the modern singers, for they now have two modes, perfect and imperfect, and the same with measure.

And so, according to the moderns, the perfect mode has a perfect measure which is assembled from longs [consisting] of three perfect tempora. But in the same mode, longs can be divided into breves, and breves into semibreves, provided that they are reduced to perfect longs, as though to one's own foundation, by means of the appropriate equivalent.

Also, there is an imperfect mode of perfect measure which is made up of longs [consisting] of perfect tempora, writing two *rectae breves* or their equivalents [i.e., rests] for such a long, or semibreves, on the basis of equivalence. And if a breve or semibreves equivalent to that breve were always joined to such an imperfect long, as the ancients did, then such a mode would be perfect and of perfect measure.

Also, according to the moderns, there is an imperfect mode of the same measure, that is the imperfect [measure], which uses imperfect longs of two imperfect tempora. But the ancients have not used such imperfections in notes, in tempora, modes, or measures.

Now since according to Franco, whose arrangement I observe here, the sounds of the said modes are the cause and first principle. And of those notes or figure signs, some things must be said here about the figures or notes by which measurable songs are notated.

<Chapter 20. What is a note or figure of measurable music according to the ancients.>

Some things have now been said about measure, about tempus and about modes. Let us consequently say something about the figures or notes of measurable music, about their values and properties, so that it may become apparent in which things the moderns distinguish themselves from the ancients.

For it is not our intention to surrender this new art of measurable music, but rather, as mentioned above, to uphold the ancient [art] as a rational one. Sometimes, therefore, certain of the statements of the ancients are repeated here, and sometimes also certain objections to the statements of the ancients, so that it may become apparent which ones are said more reasonably.

First, then, let us consider some things which the ancients have said about musical figures, and secondly certain things which the moderns [have said].

With regard to the first, let us discuss what is a musical figure, and how it should be distinguished according to the ancients. *Figura*, as magister Franco says, *is the representation of a sound that is arranged in one of the modes.* He does not say that a figure is the sound itself, but rather "the representation of a sound," in that the sign of a sound that is arranged in one of the modes represents that which is signified, in the first, namely, second and third, and thus also the others of which we have spoken, because every regular measurable song seems to be belong wholly or partly under one of those modes.

Aristoteles is very much in agreement with the said description, for he says: *Figura is the representation of sound according to its mode.* A figure, then, which is the note of the measurable art, is the representation of a sound or voice, that is, a representative sign of that voice.

Now the said teachers speak in a general sense, and do not say here what would be the shape of that representative note or figure of sound. But they do specify this afterwards, when they deal with the species of figures or notes, that is, with the long, breve, and semibreve. For figures of this kind have a quadrilateral form, because that is more suited and more easy for the notation of such songs. Whence plain music also uses them more, even though this was not the case in ancient times. But measurable music assigns diverse names, meanings, and properties, to figures of this kind.

For a modern teacher says that *the note is a quadrilateral figure of numbered sound that is measured in tempora and signifies at pleasure.* Now according the said description, it does not seem that a musical note carries continuous tempus but rather discrete [tempus], since continuous tempus does not measure numbered sound. Also, when he says "of numbered sound," it does not seem that the said general description [applies] to every musical note, for it does not seem to apply to the *semibrevis minima* which the moderns commonly say is indivisible. And when he says "signifying at pleasure," then this is true before the assigning [of its name and meaning] and in the act of assigning, but not after. For the ancients have assigned both the names and different meanings to the notes, which [notes] we shall discuss.

Now all notes of measurable music resemble each other with regard to form, in that they [all] have a quadrangular shape. Yet they are [also] distinct, because certain [notes] have straight and obtuse angles and sharp ones, after the manner of a lozenge. And they carry certain of their lines or tails in different ways, as we will explain, and others not, as shall be apparent, and according to the moderns, some are equilateral and some not. But there does not seem to be a need for equilaterality among them, as will be discussed below, nor have the ancients said any such thing.

<Chapter 21. The distinction between musical figures or notes according to the ancients.>

Some figures, as Franco says, *are singular, and some* [are] *composite,* [the latter of] *which are called ligature* (and of this we will say only few things here, because the moderns seldom use it, except in their tenors). Now *there are three more principal species* <called> *by these names: long, breve, and semibreve.*

The first of these, that is, the long, comprises three [kinds of] longs according to the ancients, namely the perfect long, the imperfect, and the *duplex*. The perfect long is said to be the fount and origin of all figures or notes of this art, and therefore *it is called perfect because it is measured in three* perfect *tempora*. For the *ternary number*, according to Franco, is called *the most perfect* in this art, *for the reason that it has taken its name from the highest Trinity, which is true and pure perfection*. Now *this quadrangular figuration is* of straight angles, *having a descending tail in the right-hand part*, thus: ▐; and its said tail represents length. *Yet the imperfect long* is named after *"in"* which means "not" and "perfect," in other words, "not perfect," either because *it contains two* equal *tempora*, or *because it is never found*, as Franco says, *without the support of a preceding of following breve*, or of semibreves that are equivalent to a breve. *For this reason*, according to the same [author], *those who call it "recta" are mistaken, since that which is "recta" can stand on its own*. And those who notate it by itself alone, without a breve, or its equivalent, preceding of following (as the moderns do when they use imperfects) seem to be even more mistaken. For [the imperfect long] has kinship with the perfect long with regard to form; for it has a figure very similar to it, namely this: ▐.

One speaks of *duplex longa*, true to its name, when [a note] is worth two longs that are not imperfect, because the ancients did not posit such a duplex long, but two perfect longs and thus six perfect tempora. Now this [*duplex longa*] is related to the perfect long with respect to its shape, except in that the length of its body exceeds the width of the other, as here: ▀ . This figure or note is not essential to this art, nor to plain music, but the authors have adopted it from geometry as one of the [musical] notes, as Aristoteles says, lest *plain music be broken during the arranging of the tenor*, as when two notes are made out of one note of plain song. And accordingly, those who use the *duplex longa* somewhere else than in tenors taken from plain song, are mistaken, for the reason why we must use it is absent [in places other than tenors].

The note or figure of the breve is distinguished in *recta* and *altera*. One speaks of *brevis recta* or *perfecta* when [a note] signifies one tempus, or an integral [whole] that is divisible into two unequal parts, or into three equal ones that are not divisible any further – unlike what has been often stated.

Another [breve] is called *altera brevis*, and it contains two *rectae breves* and is thus divisible into two equal parts, not in three. The [*brevis*] *altera* is therefore different from the *brevis recta* or *perfecta*. For it has kinship with the latter with regard to form or figure, and also with regard to fellowship, since it is not notated without the latter. So they agree with respect to form because either figure has a quadrangular rectangle, without any line, thus: ■ . Now one speaks of "without any line," because a line is not [part] of its essence (otherwise it could not exist without a line), and in this regard, among others, it is different from the long, which can never exist without a line.

Yet neither is the line altogether repugnant to the breve, as can be seen in plicas. Yet it is plicated on the left side relative to its longer plica; the long however on the right side. Now the *brevis altera* has the same meaning as the imperfect long, because both contain two perfect tempora, yet it is disitnguished from [the latter] with respect to name and shape, for one is called a long, and the other a breve; one needs a tail, but the other does not, nor without reason. They are different in that one, which is worth two tempora, should be called long when it is joined to a single perfect breve, but short with respect to the perfect long or *duplex* [long].

The moderns do not seem to notate the *brevis altera* at all, but they divide the breve into perfect breve and imperfect breve; which imperfect breve the ancients do not notate in the form of a breve, and we will speak about this below. But first something has been said about that imperfect breve.

Here follows [a dissussion] of the semibreve. According to the ancients, the semibreve is a quadrangular note that has a form [consisting] of obtuse angles in the manner of a lozenge, without any line, thus: ♦. Now according the ancients, [the semibreves] can be distinguished into major semibreve and minor. The major semibreve contains within itself two parts of the perfect or *recta brevis*. But the minor semibreve contains the third part of the perfect or *recta brevis*. And thus the major semibreve is worth two minor semibreves. Now even though they are different in value, they do agree with respect to form or shape, namely the [shape] which has just been given.

It is true that the moderns distinguish semibreves in a different way, name it, and caudate some of them, in a different way, as we will observe. Also, they do not notate the major semibreve in the form of a semibreve, but give it the shape of a breve, and they call that breve imperfect.

It is to be noted, therefore, that although according to the ancients there are only seven single notes, like the *duplex longa*, the perfect long, the imperfect long, the perfect breve and the *brevis altera*, the major semibreve and the minor semibreve, those [notes] do not all correspond to different figures, because the perfect long and the imperfect long are identical with respect to shape, similarly the *brevis recta* and *brevis altera*, and similarly the major and minor semibreve. This notwithstanding, it is sufficiently apparent from their treatises how they are distinguished from each other.

<Chapter 22. Concerning the single figures which are called plicas.>

Now there are, as Franco says, *certain other single figures which are called plicas, signifying the same things as the aforesaid* [notes] *and called by the names of the same, with the addition of this expression: "plica, plicas."*

For the plica is a sign of the division of a sound creating through low and high from that note, as Aristoteles says, *by a semitone, by a whole tone, by a minor third, by a major third, by a fourth or fifth.* And according to the same: *This plica is made subtly by the voice through the composition of the epiglottis with a repeated striking of the throat,* and it seems that the *longa plica* occurs both in plain song and in measured [song]. Thus, plicas are notated in one as well as in the other. Some plicas are ascending, some descending; also, some plicas are long, others breve.

About the semibreve, as Franco says, *we do not intend to say anything at present, for a plica semibrevis cannot be found among the single figures.* He says this because he did not posit that single semibreves, that is, those notated by themselves, can be plicated, just as they are not divisible either. For the plica is a sign of division of sound of the note to which it is attached. But in semibreves that are joined together or ligated, as far as the order of semibreves is concerned, one can find the plica, but it does not serve one semibreve but more, namely two, as here:

The ascending *longa plica*, whether there shall be a perfect long or an imperfect long or a *duplex longa*, is a quadrangular figure carrying an ascending line only on the right side, thus: : ↵, ↵ ; or more properly two, of which the one on the right should be longer than the one on the left, thus: ⌐ , ⌐. The descending perfect *longa plica*, [or the] imperfect or *duplex*, has two lines, the one on the right [is] longer than the one on the left, thus: ⌐ , ⌐.

And Aristoteles says that if it be a *plica longa perfecta, then it keeps two tempora in the note-body, another in the note-members,* that is, in the plica or in the bending; but if it shall be an *imperfect long, then it keeps one tempus in the note-body, another in the note-members.*

The ascending *plica brevis*, whether it shall be a *recta brevis* or a *brevis altera*, is a quadrangular rectangle figure which has two ascending little lines, the one on the left longer than the one on the right, thus: ⌐.

But the descending *plica brevis* similarly has two lines, of which the one on the left is longer than the one on the right, thus: ⌐.

We have discussed the names, meanings, [and] figurations of the single notes or figures of this art, which have been bequeathed to us by the ancients who grounded us in this art, in these things and others. And they have committed them to their treatises in order that these these things would be more firmly established and more durable, and thus they assigned clearly-defined and delimited meanings to the said notes, in order that, no matter how little would be taken from or added to any of them, their name, meaning, and figuration would vanish – for example, that the perfect long should signify perfect tempus, that it should be divisible into a perfect breve and a *brevis altera*, or in three perfect breves, or semibreves that make up the same value as them. For if anything be taken from or added to their said meaning, no matter how small, then one takes away their name, meaning, and figuration, so that one cannot call it a perfect long [anymore]. And the same is to be understood about the said other notes of this art.

Now these single notes were sufficient for the ancients, who have made so many beautiful and distinguished works in measurable song. They might also be sufficient for modern singers, if [only] it were prompted and not hindered by this [speculative] prying, this wantonness, and vanity, if it is permitted to say so. And if the moderns would add some things that would support the things said by the ancients, it might be tolerable. But this is not the case, in this [they are] not observing well their protestations.

Consequently, then, let us consider some things which the moderns say regarding the musical notes of this art.

<Chapter 23. The distinction between long notes with respect to [their] names and meanings, according to the moderns.>

One modern teacher asks: *How many accidental properties are there to a figure?* He answers: *One – What [is it]? Only meaning.*

This is open to question, for it seems, firstly, that there is not just one accidental property to the musical figure, but many, whether by "accidental" we understand *that which is present or absent without corruption of the subject*, or as *the higher affects* its *lower*, or conversely, as *it is distinguished by itself, or conversely by itself in the <first>* [mode]. It is possible to demonstrate these things, yet I will leave off doing so.

Secondly, "meaning" does not seem to be an accidental property of the figure of music, for [meaning] is included in its very definition, even according to this teacher, because its very purpose is to convey numbered sound in some way or other. Otherwise, unless it signified something, it would not be a note of mensural music.

Yet thereafter he asks: *How many meanings of figures are there?* He answers: *Five. – Which? Maximas, longas, breves, semibreves, and minims.* Elsewhere this teacher calls the meanings of the said figures "parts of pronunciation," [namely] where he says: *How many <parts of pronuntiation> are there? Five. – Which? Maxima, longa, breve, semibreve, and minim.* The members of these said distinctions seem to coincide in some respect, such as the first and the second, because one is higher than the other and is predicated by it, since every maxima is [a multiple] longa but not the other way round; likewise the fourth and the fifth, since every <semibreve> is <a multiple minim> but not the other way round. Therefore the division of notes [posited by] the ancients, [that is,] into long, breve, and semibreve, seems more proper. For in [that division], one member is not predicated by another.

The maxima, according to the said teacher, *is bipartite; it is called either longest or longer. What is "longest"?* [It is] *that which is measured under one accent in three long tempora*, that is, which is worth three longas. Wherefore it is elsewhere called a *triplex longa* by the same [teacher]. *What is "the longer"?* [It is] *that which is sung under one accent in two long tempora*; wherefore it is called *the duplex longa. The longa*, according to the said teacher, *is bipartite; for it is either perfect or imperfect: the perfect longa is that which is measured under one accent in three breve tempora; and the imperfect is measured under one accent in two breve tempora.*

On the other hand, there is a certain modern teacher who posits certain other long notes which he calls *largas* or *pilosas* [lit. hairy ones].

They also posit other distinctions between single long notes. For they posit a single longa that is "perfectly perfect," [or] "perfectly imperfect," "imperfectly perfect," "imperfectly imperfect," and those varieties apply also to duplex longas, and by the same argument [these varieties] seem to apply also to maxima longas, that is triple ones. For they call the single longa which is worth three perfect tempora "perfectly perfect;" [the one] which [is worth] two imperfect tempora "perfectly imperfect;" [the one] which is of three imperfect tempora "imperfectly perfect;" [and the one] which consists of two perfect tempora "imperfectly imperfect."

Would that this speculation had not descended into practice!

<Chapter 24. The distinction between the aforementioned notes with regard to certain shapes and degrees, according to the moderns.>

The said notes are distinguished into figures in multiple ways. For one modern teacher says that notes are varied in as many ways as there are modes and [figures]. As this same man says, some figures are equilateral, some unequilateral, some rectangular, some obtuse-angled, some caudated, some uncaudated, arranged upward or downward, dotted or not, before or after, to the right or to the left.

Yet when he applies the said differences between figures to the aforesaid notes, this teacher asserts that the maxima is figured like a quadrilateral and unequilateral rectangle with a downward or upward tail to the right, thus: ◥, ◢. He does not assign another figure to the triplex and duplex longas. However, the perfect or imperfect single longa is figured like [that] maxima, except that according to this teacher it is equilateral, like so: ◥, ◢. Other teachers, ancient as well as modern, make no mention of any necessity for the single longa to be equilateral, because in longs, breves, and semibreves, the imperfect is figured like the perfect, even according to this teacher. Yet the breve is figured like a single long, except that it is written without a tail, thus: ▪.

Now, according to this teacher, the semibreve, both small and minor, perfect as well as imperfect, is figured in quadrilateral and obtuse-angled [shape] without a tail, thus: ♦. Yet some of [the moderns] have caudated those semibreves, or another one of those [notes], in this way or that. For among the moderns there has been great dissent regarding the formation and figuration of the semibreve. Certain [teachers] syncopated some of them, but figured others half-full inside. Other [teachers] caudated them only at the lower or higher ends, sometimes drawing the line at the higher [end] directly above the semibreve, and sometimes in some other way. And others caudated the [notes] both above and beneath, and called them dragmas, since they resemble dragmas. Others caudated them not at the higher or lower ends, but at the sides or in the middle. Still others, when they figured the note which in song of perfect measure is worth two parts of the perfect breve, [did so] in the manner of a lozenge and gave it a tail at the lower end; and yet the note which has that same value in song of a different measure they notated in the form of a brevis.

In these and in many other things, then, what one person did, another rejected. And by now they practice many [different] novelties, although there is one point on which they more generally agree, namely, they caudate the minima semibrevis vertically at the upper end, thus: ↓. But those who notate semiminims or semiminors caudate them obliquely at the upper end, turning the tail towards the right, like so: ↗.

Some moderns, however, reduce the said varieties of notes to four degrees. And the first degree is defined in terms of equilateral and unequilateral; the second in terms of caudated and uncaudated; the third in terms of rectangular and obtuse-angled; the fourth in terms of obtuse-angled uncaudated or caudated.

The triplex longa, duplex longa, and single longa are placed in the first degree; [this degree] is named either thus: long, longer, longest, or thus: great, greater, greatest. In the second degree, following the names [used by] the ancients: perfect long, imperfect long, and brevis. In the third degree, just like the preceding ones: perfect breve, imperfect breve, semibreve. In the fourth degree, following the names of the preceding ones: perfect semibreve, imperfect semibreve, semibrevis minima.

In distinguishing the said degrees, the author remarks that the notes in question are named differently by others, except for the first degree which is named properly. Yet the second degree thus: longa, semilonga, breve. The third thus: breve, brevior [shorter]. semibreve. The fourth thus: major, minor, and minima semibrevis; or small, minor, minim.

And he who posits the said degrees holds that there are five species of singing which may be assigned to any one of them. One, that is, the first, [consists] wholly of perfects, or of the binary [number] followed by the number one, that is, a longa followed by a breve. The second [consists] of the number one followed by the binary number. The third is gathered from the first and second, that is, from the perfect followed by two numbers one, of which the last of the numbers one stands for the binary number in signification. The fourth the other way round. The fifth [consists] only of numbers one and their fractions.

Thus the notes of music are called here by numeral names. Some, therefore, do not convey continuous motion or tempus, at least if the thing signified is to agree with its name. Yet if the breve does [indeed] observe the principle of unity, then it shall be indivisible, and the semibreve even more so. And unity does not admit of fractions.

Yet let us now say something about the duplex longa.

<Chapter 25. That the duplex longa is not ligatable.>

It seems that the moderns posit multiple kinds of duplex longas. For they posit certain perfect ones, and certain ones they call largas, and others [which they call] imperfects. And some [moderns], in speaking of these things, hold generally that the duplex longa is ligatable. For they say: *Either it is a figure or it is not. If it is a figure, then it is ligatable.*

When Franco says: *A ligatable figure that is not ligated is blameworthy* (and one must not say that the duplex longa is not a figure), it seems that he considered the duplex longa to be not ligatable. This is evident from his definition of the ligature. *Ligature*, he says, *is the conjoining of single figures through properly arranged lines*. Yet although the duplex longa is [indeed] classed in the genus of single figures by reason of its body, since it does not require [several] distinct bodies, it may however be said to be *not-single* by reason of its name and meaning [duplex], and as such it is different from the single longa, that is, from the perfect longa or imperfect [longa] which are called single ones.

Also, while according to Franco single *longas* may be ligated, *they are not, however, blameworthy if they are not ligated in a binary ligature without propriety and with perfection*. So much the less, then, should the duplex longa be called blameworthy if it would not be ligated.

So when they say: *Either it is a figure or not*, this is true. But when they add: *If it is a figure, then it is ligatable*, then this conclusion must be rejected, since not every figure is in fact ligatable. For we do not say that a ligature is the conjoining of just any figures whatsoever, but [rather only] of single ones. And when Franco says that *a ligatable figure that is not ligated is blameworthy*, he does not speak here of every figure, but only of the ligatable kind which is the single figure. For we are dealing here with how a ligature is made. He who says that *a ligatable figure which is not ligated is blameworthy*, says also that a non-ligatable figure which is ligated is more blameworthy. Therefore, not only does he not mean to say that every figure is ligatable, but also that the ligatable need not everywhere be ligated.

<Chapter 26. That the duplex longa is not worth nine tempora.>

Yet there are some among the moderns who say that the duplex longa in perfect modus has nine tempora. For that reason they say that Franco, Petrus de Cruce, and all the others, have been in error.

For since, as this teacher says, it must be possible for any note to be triplicated in value, like, for example, the semibreve is worth three minims, breves three semibreves, [and] the long three breves, therefore the duplex longa, or rather larga, must doubtlessly [be capable of having] the value of three longas as well, that is, nine tempora.

Yet this teacher irrationally rebukes Franco, Petrus de Cruce, and other teachers who were so distinguished in their times, and whose memory is deserving of blessing. And he states in too uncivil a fashion that they were in error. Let him take heed, lest he be even more in error about many things in his own treatise, where he posits many ridiculous things, and on occasion even seems to contradict himself. Yet I will refrain from demonstrating this.

It must be pointed out, therefore, that not only must [not] every note be capable of being threefold in value, but neither in just any [value]. For the longa is not worth three longas, nor the breve three breves, nor the semibreve three semibreves. Yet those notes do properly indicate time as [being] divisible into three equal parts. Now if the duplex longa were to be triplicated in value in perfect modus, then it shall be worth not just nine tempora but eighteen, because it shall be worth three duplex longas, that is, six single ones; which no person would say.

Nor is it true of every note that it may signify time as [being] divisible into three equal parts. For this is repugnant to the perfect longa, [and] to the altera or imperfect breve, [and] to the minor or imperfect and minima semibrevis, and likewise also to the duplex longa. For if the duplex longa were to be triplicated in such a way that it would be worth three longas, then it shall no longer be a duplex longa, but rather a triplex. In this way it will lose both its name and its meaning.

Now the ancients would certainly have discussed the triplex longa if they had wanted to. Yet they did not consider [that note] necessary to this art, probably because of the reasons mentioned before. Yet they did posit the duplex longa for good reason, and since it does not go back to the primary origin of the notes of this art, the moderns say many things about it which the ancients never said.

And the said teacher posits certain duplex largas of which we should say something right away.

<Chapter 27. That it is irrational to notate a duplex longa that is called a larga.>

It is to be known, says the aforementioned teacher, that just as the duplex longa is diminished [imperfected] by breves, so is it enlarged by tails. Whence it is to be noted that *its body is worth so many perfections or imperfections beyond the usual measure as it contains tails or divided breves.*

And likewise further down, in the eleventh chapter of his work: *The square note*, he says, *which has a figure beyond the usual measure, that is,* [beyond] *the boundary of the duplex longa, containing several tails, be it two, or three, or more, some ascending and some* <descending>, *or containing within itself divided breves, is called a larga, as in the following* [example]:

For this teacher posits duplex longas which he calls largas, or split ones, and he caudates them with many tails, not just at the outer ends but also in the middle, going up or down.

If only he had called such things by their [true] name, [that is,] monstruous things. For we are dealing with a monster when something contains more than is proper to its usual nature, just as there is a defect in [its] nature when it has less. For square notes are customarily caudated only at their extreme ends or angles, and never in the middle. Oh, what abuse, what illegality, what vanity, what insolence, what inutility, what coarseness! Oh, what presumption in figures of notes, what confusion! Cannot one say ironically about things like these what Aristotle said about the Ideas against Plato: *Let such* notes *rejoice, for they are illusory things* [lit. monsters]?

Also, this teacher holds that the duplex longa is ligatable not just in a binary ligature (where the ancients allowed only the single longa to be ligated), but even in a ternary ligature. This teacher ligates the duplex longa in a binary ligature together with a breve:

and in a ternary ligature, notating it in the middle between two breves, in the following manner:

This author, it must be said, ligates the duplex longa in irrational fashion. For this is [not] proper to it, as demonstrated above, especially in a threefold ligature, since, according to the ancients as well as other moderns, all middle notes are breves unless they are joined together in the opposite propriety which semibreviates the first two, or shows them to be semibreves.

And yet this teacher imputes to the old art that it already knew the said manner of notation, namely, [that] in which the breve is ligated together with a duplex longa or with two breves. For he says in the eighth chapter of his work: *We see in the old art that, when a single breve is ligated to a duplex longa, then that duplex longa is worth only five tempora, and when two breves are conjoined to it at either side, it is worth four tempora. This is just as true in the new art, because the single longa,* et cetera.

Yet it must be said that the said manner of notation, in which the duplex longa is ligated with a breve, or breves, is found neither in the art of Aristoteles, nor in the art of Franco, who seem to be the principal ancient teachers who have dealt with measurable music. For Franco says: *Those who ligate three longas together in some place, as for example in tenors, are vehemently in error; the same is true of those who ligate a longa in between two breves, for with regard to the notation of the middle ones, as said before, all should be breviated.* And when Franco speaks of the single longa, if thus he reproves those who ligate it between two breves, then how much more would he have reproved those who would ligate a duplex longa between two breves.

This teacher, who professes to expound the old and new arts in his work, ought to rehearse faithfully which things are of the old [art] and which of the new, [and] not impute to the old things they did not say at all. Yet let those who have diligently examined the works on this subject by the ancients and moderns judge whether he takes proper care to do this.

And yet, perhaps the said teacher means by "old" some art which deals with the new manner of singing and notating. For there has been such diversity [of opinion] among the moderns that the earlier ones might [already] be called "old" from the viewpoint of the others.

Nor should one posit, rationally speaking, that a duplex longa could be imperfected by a breve, or by breves that are separate from it or ligated to it, nor similarly by a semibreve [separate] from it, or by a minim [separate] from it, as we will see below.

<Chapter 28. That imperfect duplex longas are not necessary to this art.>

I say, moverover, that imperfect duplex longas of four perfect tempora, or of four imperfect [tempora], are not necessary to this <art>, because there is no need for a duplex longa that is worth two single perfect longas, and hence even less for the imperfect duplex longa. For this is to confuse perfections, and also to confuse measures, nothing else.

For [the longa] itself, being perfect, can stand on its own, or together with another one similar to itself, and thus the perfections and the measure are in no way confused. Not so the imperfect duplex [longa]. Now what prevents measurable songs from being notated without it, as the ancients did, who made so many beautiful and good songs? For they never used the imperfect duplex [longa]. And not only does the imperfect duplex longa seem unnecessary, but [it seems] irrational as well. For it is irrational in any art to posit something that is not only unnecessary to that art, but conflicts with the very foundation of that art.

With respect to the art of measurable music, this is true of the imperfect duplex longa, because that whole art, as the ancients held (and some moderns state as well), is founded in perfection, since the ternary number, as far as the species of [measurable] music is concerned, is considered not only perfect, but most perfect [of all]. That which conflicts with the measure, therefore, [that] which conflicts with perfection, appears to be posited irrationally in this art.

The same is not true of the imperfect single longa, for it is immediately restored to perfection by the breve joined to it before or after, or by semibreves that are equivalent to a breve, without which [breve], or without which [semibreves], it is never found to occur.

<Chapter 29. That single imperfect longas of imperfect tempora are repugnant to this art, and likewise also songs put together from such imperfects.>

According to the moderns, as we have seen, the species of the single longa is fourfold: some are called "perfectly perfect," some "perfectly imperfect," some "imperfectly perfect," [and] some "imperfectly imperfect." Of these, the old posited only the first and last species. The first they called, in a single term, a perfect longa, and the other an imperfect longa. They did not posit the other two intermediate ones, since these do not seem to be necessary to this art.

Now a science or discipline is concerned with things that are necessary; and that which is [not] rooted in perfection, as already said, seems to conflict with this art. However, just like what we said about the imperfect duplex longa, single imperfect <longas> of this kind disturb and confuse the perfection, and likewise the measure.

Not so the imperfect longa, which the ancients have posited in the manner in which they used them. For it hinders neither perfection nor measure, since it always has perfection connected with it. Therefore, according to the ancients, a song is never put together from imperfects, but perfection follows perfection without confusion where it is notated, and perfections not only begin in the notes but end as well.

But this is not the case with the other imperfect longs. For with these [notes], perfection does not follow perfection in clear and unconfused manner (ternary [number following] ternary), but rather imperfection (binary [number following] binary). That is why perfections neither begin nor end in the notes.

The ancients never did this. On the contrary, they so much detested songs of this kind, that is, [songs] put together from imperfects, that they called them impossible—by which they did not understand that they are impossible simply as existing in actual fact (for in actual fact both good and bad things, rational as well irrational things, can indeed exist), but they said that those songs are impossible perhaps according to that common saying: "We are only able to do that which we can do in accordance with law and art." For those songs go against the art, which is founded in perfection.

Yet the moderns say that in songs [made] out of imperfects, all things are ultimately brought back to [the basis of] equality. Therefore the moderns hold that the imperfect thing, or song, is just as possible as the perfect. But in that case another statement by the same teacher does not seem to be tenable, [namely,] when he says that there is an imperfect modus of perfect measure and a perfect modus of imperfect measure.

<Chapter 30. That songs made from perfects are appropriately compared to the highest Trinity.>

Yet the said teacher struggles so hard to justify imperfect notes, and songs put together from imperfects, that he seems to rebuke the ancients for comparing natural song made out of perfects to the highest Trinity.

For he says that before God assumed human flesh, except in God's essence, it was possible for song of imperfects to exist. Also, since God is threefold in persons, in the same way as he is in one in substance, natural song need not be related to the divine Trinity more than to Unity [i.e. oneness]. Also, whether one sings in perfects or in imperfects, God is neither more nor less threefold and one [for that reason].

Yet we must say that one should not rebuke those who compare song put together from perfects to the highest Trinity. For every principle is appropriately related back to that from which it effectively and exemplarily originated, just as all good [is appropriately related back] to the first Good which is the good in essence, other things [being good only] by partaking [in the first Good]: every truth [partaking] in the first Truth which is God, and all existence in the first Existence, and all being in the first Being. For all multitude proceeds from the One, and all being from the first Being which is the Being of God. From this, accordingly, is derived [all] existence in other things, in *some more directly, in others more obscurely*.

Every perfection proceeds from the highest and first Perfection, and consequently every ternary number, trinity, or ternareity relates back, by reason of the perfection which it lawfully carries, to the first, highest, and most perfect Trinity. So, when they say that before God assumed flesh from the Virgin, song from imperfects could exist, it must be said that this is true only as a matter of [historical] fact, not in congruence with the foundations of this art, which is rooted in perfection through the rationale of the ternary number.

Yet what is the purpose of speaking of the Word incarnate? For both before and after that ineffable assumption of human nature by the Person of the Word, God truly was three and one, and this from time everlasting, and he shall be forever without end. And when a song from perfects is related back to to the highest, first, and most perfect Trinity by reason of the ternary [number], then this is not true of song from imperfects, since there is absolutely no imperfect thing that agrees, or can agree, with that highest Trinity.

Yet they go on to say: "God is three in persons, just as he is one in substance, [therefore] natural song made out of perfects need not be compared to the divine Trinity more than to its Unity." It must be replied that natural song put together from perfects is compared to both to the divine Trinity and to its Unity; to the Trinity by reason of perfection and of the separateness which is conveyed by the ternary [number], but to that Unity by reason of the concord which is required in songs of this kind. For concord is defined as the concord of distinct pitches or distinct songs reduced into one. And in that highest Trinity there is the highest concord, in which abides the most onefold Unity of that same divine essence.

Then they say: "Whether one sings in perfects or in imperfects, God is no less three and one." This is true, since God is so truly and actually perfect within himself that there is nothing outside himself, that is, no creature whatsoever, to which he could be compared in actual reality, or could depend in actual reality, or by which he could be regulated.

Therefore we can truly say: "Whether there be nothing outside himself or something [outside himself], whether you or anyone else acts well and virtuously, or whether you sin badly and wickedly, or [whether there be] any other change or difference in creatures, he in himself is not changed in any respect." *For I*, says the Prophet, *am the Lord, I change not*. And the Blessed Jacob, *with whom is no variableness, neither shadow of turning*. And Boethius: *resting unmoved, putting all things in motion. In nothing is He less three and one*.

For between good and perfect deeds and bad and imperfect [deeds] there is a great difference, great variation, as compared to each other and to God. For he approves and rewards the former, and punishes and reproves the latter, since he is the cause of good things, and not of bad things. *Further*, says Plato in the Timaeus, *of no evil he is the cause*, which is to be understood about the evil of guilt, whatever may be [true] of the evil of penalty through which something is brought back to the good of justice. Whence, according to that Gospel of the Blessed John, *All things are made by him, and without him nothing is made*. Says the Blessed Augustine: *Sin, indeed, was not made by him; for sin is nothing, and men become nothing when they sin*, namely of the genus of which the Apostle speaks when he says: *If I do not have Charity, I am nothing*. And Boethius in [his] book of the Consolation: *Sin*, he says, *is nothing, since he who can do all things cannot make it*. Also, sin is called "nothing" not by reason of the deed in which it is subjectively founded or of an evil will by which we sin. For according to the Blessed Augustine, *sin is the evil that we commit, but punishment the evil which we suffer*. Rather, sin is called "nothing" by reason of privation and a turning away from God.

To talk about this with sophistication, however, is another undertaking.

<Chapter 31. That it is not necessary for the single longa to be equilateral.>

We have said a number of things about the single longas which the moderns add to those posited by the ancients, with regard to both their names and their meanings. Now let us say some things about them with regard to their figurations. If [every] particular figure would correspond to a particular note name and meaning, then we would have many more figures of notes than we do, even of single longas, for according to the moderns these are many. Yet there is only one figure that corresponds to [all] those longas, both those that are perfect and those that are imperfect. For, as we have seen above, it is figured in quadrangular, rectangular, and equilateral [shape], and caudated either upward or downward on the right-hand side.

Yet although a figure of this kind may be appropriate to the single longa, in that it helps to distinguish it from the duplex [longa] by means of an equilateral figure, or [may be appropriate] to the single perfect longa—and inequilaterality [appropriate] to the imperfect [longa], in order to distinguish them from each other, namely, inequilaterality in which the sides of longitude are greater that the sides of latitude, just the opposite of the duplex longa—it does not however seem necessary for the single perfect or imperfect longa to be equilateral. The ancients did not posit this, and similarly neither do all the moderns, since difficulty of notation must be avoided wherever conveniently possible. What seems essential, and [what seems] to suffice in the figure of the single longa, is that it be a quadrilateral [and] rectangular one, whose latitude does not exceed [its] longitude, even though [a note] caudated downward or upward on the right-hand side could not truly achieve equilaterature [in any case]. And this is to be understood also about the figure of the breve, namely, that it is not necessary for it to be equilateral. And again it is to be understood about the semibreve, for equilaterality is not necessary to it.

<Chapter 32. That the imperfect breve is not necessary to this art.>

The moderns distinguish a recta brevis and an imperfect one; the ancients posited the first, but not the second. Now if division must be through opposites, and one of [those opposites] is a recta brevis, then the other is not a recta brevis, and indeed not properly [called] a recta brevis, for with regard to its primary application which it had from old [or: from the ancients], it is not a breve, nor must it be so called, but rather a <semibreve>. For according to [the moderns], if some [note] is to be a breve and to have the form of a breve, then it must signify that the integral and perfect tempus is divisible, namely, into either three equal parts or two unequal ones; and that it conveys two such tempora inasmuch as it is an altera brevis.

But if something conveys more or less, then it must have neither the name nor the form of the breve. Therefore some moderns speak irrationally, and they take great care that in practice the form of the breve may not be changed in any note as long as it contains more than the third part of a perfect tempus. And therefore, since the major semibreve which the ancients posited is worth more than the third part of the perfect breve, they give it the form of a breve and thus change a semibreve into a breve. Yet since [these notes] should be distinguished in more respects than species, they do not keep their own protestations as well as they say.

One must know that the figures of all the long and short notes remain the same today as [they were] handed down in ancient times by Franco. And from the things that have been said above it is evident that the note in question should not have the form of a breve but of the semibreve, because neither the name nor the form of the whole agrees with the part. And if they show this to be true of the minor part of that recta brevis, which is its third part, why do they not show this to be true also of its major part, since neither the major nor the minor part receives the name or the form of the whole? And just as the duplex or single imperfect longas, which were not posited by the ancients, are not necessary to this art, as we have said above, so it seems to be the case with the imperfect breve which signifies a tempus divisible into two equal parts, not three. Now this breve has [the status of] imperfection because it encloses tempus divisible in two parts, not three. Yet because of this it also encloses another imperfection, since the tempus which is enclosed by tempus is imperfect—of which the ancients have never spoken. Accordingly, although [the ancients] have posited the first kind of imperfection, albeit only in the single longa with which tempus perfectum stands, they never posited the other kind. We have said above certain things about this imperfect breve. And the things said about it both then and now are sufficient. Let us proceed with semibreves.

<Chapter 33. Brief prologue touching upon the intention and the order of the things that are to be said.

Let us then move on to the semibreves, to whose doctrine the moderns devote no small effort. Indeed they labor greatly over the distinction, meaning, value, and naming of them. And even though one should say more about notes that are more pertinent to this art, like longs and breves, and less about those which [are] less, like semibreves which seem less pertinent to the art, some moderns do the exact opposite.

Many are the proceedings, many the chapters, which they devote to [semibreves]. They make great use of them, and because of them they greatly expand their new art, their manner of singing and of notating songs. They exalt them with names, decorate them with plicas or tails in manifold ways. And although active or passive qualities should follow the form or species of a thing, they ascribe to them many qualities which do not seem appropiate to them (in which they should be governed by longs and breves if their original and primary meaning were to be preserved), even if *nothing can act beyond its species*, wherefore they attribute to them [the power] to imperfect duplex longas, and single ones, and breves, and one another.

Yet among the things they say about them, and which they attribute to them, there are some, it seems, which should be weighed more. And let the first of those things be [the claim] that the semibreve is divisible through a division of the integral whole. Second, that the semibreve is caudatable. Third, that it may be notated by itself, without another semibreve beside it. Fourth, that it can imperfect longas, breves, and one the other. The ancients never posited any of those things about semibreves. Let us show, therefore, lest they be thought remiss for that reason, that these things are not to be posited about semibreves [at all].

And firstly let us speak of the second, since we have already considered the first above. And let us proceed with the second in this way: first, that it is repugnant to the semibreve to be caudated or plicated; second, that if it would be caudated, this is less appropriate to the semibrevis minima than to the others; third, that if it would be caudated, it ought to be caudated at the left and right angles rather than the higher or lower ones.

<Chapter 34. That the moderns caudate semibreves in irrational fashion.>

The moderns, as we have said many times, caudate certain semibreves nowadays (I say "certain" now, such as minims and semiminims). Those who posit these things have sometimes caudated just about all [of them], albeit in different ways. Yet they do this merely in deed, for the line or tail seems repugnant not just to the nature of a semibreve notated by itself, but also to its figure. And let us demonstrate this plausibly according to what arises and what the matter permits, relying in this on the aforementioned foundations and statements of the ancients.

We argue thus: to that singly-notated note to which it is repugnant to be divided in a division of the integral whole, it is [also] repugnant to be caudated or plicated. For as we have seen above, the tail or plica is a sign of division, or of upward or downward inflection of the sound of the note to which it is attached. And since a sign and that which is signified must agree, the tail or plica may be attached only to what is divisible, since it is a sign of division. Yet division is repugnant to the semibreve, as demonstrated above.

Moreover, confusion in the distinction of note values, and difficulty in figuring where it serves no purpose, are to be avoided. Just this is the case, however, even according to some moderns, with the plication of semibreves that are notated by themselves. For one of them speaks thus:

> *What is one to say if someone argued that all notes, of whatever genus or species they may be — duplex and single longas, perfect and imperfect, prima and altera breves of both perfect or imperfect tempus, or major, minor, and minima semibreves, if is it proper so to call them — do not require new signs, figures, or lines, [or] superfluous plicas, since every measurable song can be performed both slow and fast, and the value of all the notes known more succinctly, without plicas and lines? Indeed the confusion of different lines hinders every singer, even a fluent one, by not allowing him to sing, in sounds uttered without delay, a song that [he has] not otherwise seen [and which is] riddled with different lines and plicas. For the eye of the singer, looking and retaining equally, is led astray*

> because of the figuration, invention being destroyed at last. For the precise figuration of notes was invented in order that the singer, who was at first unsure of the value of [those notes], could relax because the figuration was fully notated, and would no longer be unable to sing, because uncertainty had been removed.

These are the words of the author who thereupon says: *What should I say in response to the said argument? I do not find . . ., and I would for the most part have agreed with the same man, following the old, if the power of use did not prevent it.* Yet with all respect to this teacher, the excusation does not persuade. For nothing ought to be notated irrationally in the art, no irrational custom ought to be sustained in the art. A power that is irrational seems tyrannical; a bad custom is to be abolished, and no amount of time should [be allowed to] foster a bad and irrational custom that goes against good custom [and] precept.

It seems they imitate those vain Athenians to whom novelties were so pleasing. Yet one must not praise, one must not approve, it would appear, that a custom which goes against the founders of an art is observed, by people who profess to be observing that art, only because of its novelty; they should look for such reasons as shall color and sustain such use.

Franco, they say, prohibits the plication of semibreves since the perfect breve divides either into three equal semibreves that cannot be divided any further, or into two unequal [semibreves]. Not so the moderns, for they hold that any of the three in which the perfect breve is divided can be further divided into three. Yet according to [Franco], there was no need for semibreves to be plicated in this way, because their [combined] value can be expressed in a small number; and [that value] could be determined well enough without plicas.

It has to be said here, first, that Franco prohibits the plication of semibreves not because of this, but rather for the reason that has already been mentioned. Second, it must be said that however many semibreves beyond three one could notate for the recta brevis, even up to nine as we have seen, as did some of the old who followed the art of Franco, it does not follow from this that semibreves are plicatable. Nor did those ancients who notated more than three semibreves for a perfect tempus ever plicate one. Moreover, according to that argument, divisible notes would be the more principally plicatable ones, and accordingly, minims and semiminims either should not be plicated, or at least less so than the other semibreves from which they are different.

Now they say: according to the ancients it was not necessary to plicate semibreves, for when they notated two unequal semibreves for a perfect breve, they would usually make the first one shorter, and the second longer, moved perhaps by the imitation of nature which is more vigorous in the end than in the beginning. Yet the moderns say that this is not necessary, since it may also be done the other way round, namely, that the first semibreve would be made longer than the second, like they do nowadays. To distinguish [the two notes], therefore, one would have to say that the altera [brevis] may be plicated. And they also say that art need not always imitate nature.

It is true that of two unequal semibreves the first can be made major and the second minor, just as the opposite [is true]. Yet it seems more proper for the minor to come first, and then the major, as the ancients did, for even though art may not imitate nature, it must however imitate it as much as possible. Nor does it follow that if the first of the said semibreves is nowadays made longer, one would have to plicate the altera in order to distinguish them. Here they apply the fallacy of the consequence from many indetermined causes [being reduced] to one [cause], since [those semibreves] may also be distinguished from each other in another [way] or other ways. And since the ancients distinguished them, after [their] custom, without tails, then why can the moderns not distinguish them from each other in [their own] contrary custom, so that they would not ascribe to [those notes] things that are not appropriate to them?

Still, here one may say that when the ancients wanted to sing that span of time which is [now] conveyed by the major semibreve, or that [span] which [is conveyed] by a minor [semibreve], they notated in fast measure an imperfect longa for the major semibreve, a breve for the minor, and a perfect longa for them both [together], as is apparent in the following duplex hocket.

[Example on pp. 57 and 58]

The first part of the said song, namely that which is upon the text *A l'entrade* etc., appears to represent [a notational alternative] to song put together from two unequal semibreves with the minor coming before the major; the second, upon the second text *Plaingnant*, to that [song] which [is put together] the other way round.

Now since there are four species of notes in the song notated here, namely, perfect long, imperfect long, brevis recta, and semibreve, someone who would want to notate [the song] in the manner of notating of the moderns, should write [1] the semibreve which they call parva for the perfect long, [2] the semibreve which they call minor for the imperfect long, [3] the minima semibrevis for the brevis recta, and [4] a semiminim for the semibreve notated [here]. For as far as the thing is concerned [that is, the actual temporal duration], the said notes seem to be similar in value and measure, no matter what names they may have. And if that is so, then the moderns should not boast that they have invented "minims" and "semiminims" [i.e., new names for old things]; for one should care more about the thing than about names.

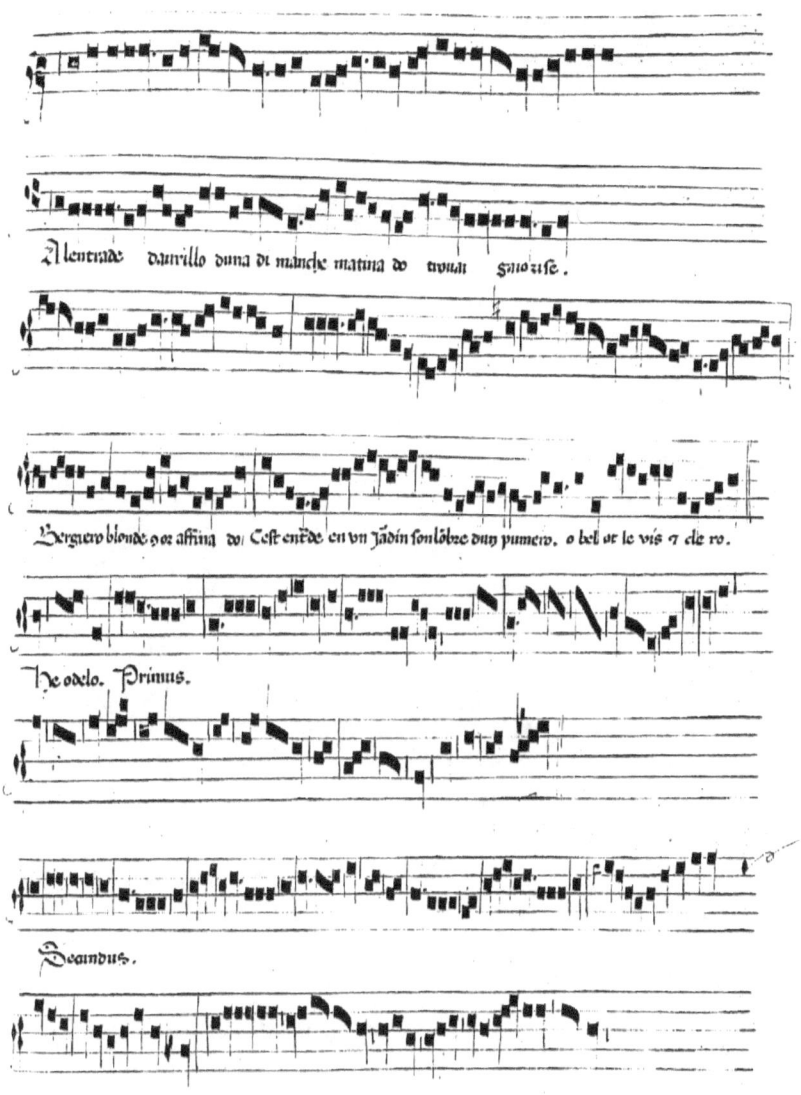

Paris, Bibliothèque nationale, MS lat. 7202, fol. 287r

Paris, Bibliothèque nationale, MS lat. 7202, fol. 287v

Now in view of the said name of "minimity" it does not seem altogether rational that one should notate two semiminims for a minim. For there cannot be something that is less [minus] than the least [minimus]. Therefore the old note names seem at least somewhat more rational than the modern ones.

Furthermore, it must be said that the plica seems to be repugnant to the single semibreve, not only because of its meaning, but also because of its figure; for it is figured in the shape of a lozenge. Yet such a figure, if it is to be caudated, should be caudated either at the sharp points (that is, at the higher and lower ends), or at the obtuse ones (which are sideways). But at the sharp [points] this would not be rational, it seems, for these are in the middle between the obtuse or side ones (and a figure may not be caudated in the middle); also the figure may not be caudated at those points since they carry the rationale neither of right nor of left: this is true of the said sharp points. But neither [is it rational] at the obtuse points, since it is not customary to caudate notes of this kind at those points. It seems, then, that a semibreve notated by itself is not caudatable. I say "notated by itself" because the case is different when it is joined by another; for something that is not appropriate to one thing [may still be] appropriate to many [other] things.

<Chapter 35. That if the semibreve is to be caudated, then this is less appropriate to the semibrevis minima than to the others.>

Some, perhaps, would say that if a free-standing semibreve is to be caudated, like the moderns do in practice, then it seems less irrational to do this with the major or minor semibreve than the semibrevis minima.

First, because the major and minor semibreve are closer in value to plicatable notes [than is the semibrevis minima]. For according to the moderns, the major semibreve can be divided into three and the minor into two; *for change is easier in things that have a symbol.* Yet the minima [semibrevis], by its very name, appears to be indivisible.

Second, the major semibreve takes up a longer span of time; and the line or plica is a sign of slack pace [i.e., it cannot be used in notes that are sung too fast]. Thirdly, because *the better way is in fewer things.* And one needs to write fewer major semibreves, in a perfect or imperfect tempus, than minims. Fourth, because notators must avoid strain wherever convenient; and it would involve less strain to caudate three or two [semibreves] than six or nine. Fifth, because of the distinction to be had between them [i.e., since they are otherwise all written as untailed lozenges]. For *it is pointless to do with more what can be done with less.* After all, if, in a flock of some animals, someone wanted to distinguish one from the others, then he would mark out only that one, not all the others.

From this is would seem that minimae semibreves are either not caudatable [at all], or less so than major or minor ones. [Caudation] is to be avoided not only for the sake of eliminating confusion, but also because of the said reasons, and others that could be mentioned.

I say "for the sake of . . . confusion" because when the major or minor ones are caudated and the minims not, then there is less confusion, and not just less strain, than [when it is] the other way round. Now, at whatever points [those notes] may be caudated, whether above or below, the upper tail must not be used for the semibrevis minima, for these reasons. [1] Because in ligatures, opposite propriety pertains to semibreves, and [2] because it is not right in ligatures and single figures, and [3] because opposite propriety does not seem to pertain more to minimae semibreves than to others, and [4] because opposite propriety joins together not only notes that are shaped in the manner of a lozenge, but also square rectangular ones. Now it is not satisfactory to say that the reason why minims are caudated at the top is because they can be distinguished from others more quickly through [caudation] than through dots. For although that distinction may be quicker, it is not however more rational, as is evident from the things that have been said and will be said.

<Chapter 36. That if a lone semibreve is to be caudated, then it must be done less inappropriately, at obtuse angles rather than sharp ones.>

It may perhaps seem to some that if a singly-notated semibreve is caudatable, then it must be less inappropriate for it to be caudated at obtuse angles than sharp ones.

First, because the obtuse angles occupy the extreme ends of a figure like this. Yet the sharp [angles], that is, the higher and lower, serve the rationale of the middle between the former, in accordance with the placement and direct aspect of such a figure. For it is not customary for figures to be caudated in the middle, but rather at their extreme ends; this is evident from square rectangular figures.

Second, because the plica or tail are customarily placed [only] at those angles which serve the rationale of the right or left; this is true of the obtuse angles of the figure of the semibreve, but not the sharp ones.

Third, because the plica seems to be more appropriate to the larger angle than the smaller one, for [the larger] is closer than the smaller to the rationale of the whole and of its divisibility; for the plica is a sign of division, yet the obtuse angle is larger than the sharp one.

Fourth, because a figure, if it is to be caudated, should be caudated at the angles from which [the figure] takes its name, more so than at the others; now the figure of the semibreve is named after the obtuse angles, not the sharp ones.

Fifth, because the figure of the semibreve is caudated more reasonably, or less irrationally, at those angles from whose caudation arise more distinctions between semibreves. This is true of the caudation of semibreves at obtuse angles, just like the tails in quadrangular rectangular figures, that is, [the figures] of long and breve notes. For the note which is to be caudated upward or downward at the right-hand side, like so: ♩ ♩ , could be called a major semibreve; but the one which [is to be caudated] downward or upward on the left-hand side like so: ♩ could be called a <minor> semibreve, in this way: ♩; and and the one which lacks a tail altogether, like so: • , [could be called] a minima.

However, I am speaking hypothetically or by supposition, not stating categorical approval that this is how it must be done—on the contrary, rejecting caudation in every kind of semibreve, at sharp sides as well as obtuse ones. And [now] I speak of those notated alone.

<Chapter 37. That the semibreve is not to be notated by itself alone without another semibreve, or others, beside it.>

The moderns notate solitary semibreves, that is, [they notate] one semibreve without another semibreve or others beside it. This seems irrational, however, for it is repugnant to a part to be placed by itself in order to complete the whole to which it belongs. For since the whole it is greater than the part, it necessarily requires more parts to constitue its whole. For it is impossible for a single part to make up the whole to which it belongs. Yet as demonstrated above, the semibreve, in relation to the right and perfect tempus, has the rationale of a part, not of the whole. Therefore none of those [parts] is by itself alone capable of making up the whole to which it belongs, but rather it needs another one, or other ones, beside itself in order to render the whole.

Also, it is repugnant to imperfection to be notated by itself. Whence the commentator Eustratius, [commenting] on the book of Ethics says: *imperfect things do not stand* [or: are not stable]. For as mentioned above, no semibreve is able to convey perfection, given that it does not have the rationale of the whole but only of the part. And the whole and the perfect are the same thing. And perfection, in measurable music, has to do with the ternary number. Yet it has already been demonstrated above that it is repugnant to the semibreve to be divided into three equal parts.

From this one can see why it is [on the other hand] appropriate for the longa or brevis to be notated by itself, without another similar note beside it. And from these things it is also apparent that it is irrational to give the form of a breve to [the note] which the moderns notate as an imperfect breve. Also it may, in some way, be on account of their form or figure that it is appropriate to notate longs and breves singly, since their figures are quadrilateral and rectangular, flat above and flat below. This is not true of the form of the semibreve, which starts above with a sharp angle and ends below in a similar [sharp angle], and hence does not possess as much firmity and stability, nor [as much] perfection, as do the figures of the longa or brevis.

For a straight angle seems more perfect than a sharp or even obtuse one. It is for this reason that the figures of the notes used in measurable music have been taken from plain music. And with respect to these properties, it is appropriate that measurable music should imitate plain music as much as possible. And in plain music, according to those who know well how to notate chant, one rarely or never finds a single semibreve unaccompanied by another similar one. But the figures of the longa and brevis are often found there without another similar one [beside them].

Yet, say the moderns, neither we nor the ancients have ever said that the semibreve is found alone, for is always found beside a longa, or beside a breve, or beside another semibreve. Now, I grant that it is indeed appropriate to join a semibreve together with another semibreve, or others, in order to make up, or complete, the exact whole to which it belongs. For in fact the semibreve note *must* be brought together [with another note] with which, or through which, it can make up the precise whole to which it belongs, that is, the recta brevis. But this is the case only with another semibreve or other [semibreves], just as the ancients said. Now if a lone semibreve is never to be placed beside a breve, then so much the less may it be placed beside a single or duplex longa. Nor did the ancients ever maintain that a single semibreve can imperfect or perfect a breve or longa. And in what follows we must deal with imperfections.

<Chapter 38. What the moderns say about the imperfections of musical notes.>

Regarding the matter of imperfections let us proceed as follows: First, we shall deal with certain things which they call imperfections. Second, we shall object to imperfections of this kind. Third, we shall respond to some of the arguments with which the moderns endeavor to affirm the imperfections which they posit in notes.

With regard to the first, we shall, first of all, deal briefly with some of the many things which the moderns say about imperfections in musical notes. Secondly, let us remark something about those things that are more in accord with the statements of the ancients.

As for the first, the moderns hold that there are certain notes which are imperfected by certain others, but which do not imperfect any themselves, such as longas that are either single or duplex, perfect or imperfect. Among these, the perfect longas are imperfected by the recta brevis, by the major semibreve (which, according to them, is the third part of the recta brevis), and by the minim, though the imperfection of longas is immediate [when effected] by the breve, but mediate [when effected] by semibreves. For according to them, to imperfect is to subtract or take away, from the value of the note which is to be imperfected, the [same] amount as the note which does the imperfecting is worth.

There are other notes which are not imperfected, such as minims which do however imperfect some longas and breves, and also major semibreves. Yet these are not themselves imperfected, since their value cannot be [made] less. There are other [notes] which are able to imperfect and to be imperfected in relation to different notes; and notes of this kind are recta breves and major semibreves. Yet breves, as we have said, do imperfect longas and similarly the said semibreves do imperfect longas, and the said breves are imperfected by major semibreves and by the minim, and the major semibreve by the minim. There are other notes which can neither be imperfected nor do any imperfecting, such as minor semibreves that contain two minims. These are not imperfected because they are not divisible into three equal parts, according to both common use and the [limited] ability of the human voice; yet their middle part is called indivisible, just like the minim.

No note can however be imperfected unless it, or some part of it, is divisible into three equal parts, as is the case with the imperfect single longa of two perfect tempora. Yet the said note is not capable of doing any imperfecting. For although the imperfect breve contains three semibreves, it is however only very rarely divided into them, since they would be too difficult to measure. Because of this difficulty, therefore, the minor semibreve may not imperfect the imperfect breve any more than the imperfect single longa, containing two breves, [may imperfect] the perfect duplex longa.

It is already apparent from these and many other things that the moderns posit many imperfections in notes. For example, they hold that the duplex longa [containing] imperfect tempora is imperfectible by the recta brevis, by the major semibreve, and by the minim. Similarly they also hold that the perfect single longa is imperfectible by the said three notes, the imperfect single longa [containing] perfect tempora by the major semibreve and by the minim; the imperfect longa of imperfect tempus by the minim semibreves, the perfect breve by the major semibreve and minim, the imperfect breve by the minim, [and] the major semibreve by the minim.

These and many other things the moderns say, in various different places, about imperfections in musical notes, things which the ancients never said or posited. In this regard one should note well that the moderns are inventing ways by which they oppose perfection in manifold manner, [that they] fight perfection and, in consequence, [fight] the art which is founded in perfection. In doing so they also seem to oppose the very nature of things. For a thing, by nature, seeks its perfection, and moves, by nature, from the imperfect to the perfect. For all things seek the good, and flee the bad and imperfect. Yet [the moderns never] discuss in what ways imperfection in notes might be restored to perfection, but rather in what way, and by means of what thing, the perfect may be imperfected and thus not maintain its perfection. This does not seem praiseworthy, however, but rather to be at odds with this science, nothing else.

<Chapter 39. Which things would be required in order that certain notes be capable of imperfecting others, or of being imperfected by them.>

If we suppose that imperfections in notes would be possible after the customary manner of speaking (whatever may be the case in terms of truth or the demands of appropriateness), then it may seem that they are required in order that a note may be imperfectible by another, and that they are required also in order that a note may be capable of imperfecting another.

As for the first, the note which is imperfected must, according to its meaning, carry a perfection which signifies that tempus is divisible into three equal parts. Also, in order that the note which carries the perfection (as we have said) may be capable of being imperfect, it seems necessary that it would not lose the figure [i.e. note shape] on account of its imperfectibility, but will have the same figure after it is made imperfect as it did before, when it was still perfect. For a note is not imperfected in figure, but rather in its value or meaning.

I say, moreover, that in order for a note to imperfect another, it seems necessary that it should have some sort of imperfection, in relation to the [note that is] to be imperfected. For it is proper to a perfect thing, being perfect, not to imperfect but rather to perfect. Also, if it is appropriate to a note by itself that it can imperfect another, then it seems appropriate to the same [note] that it can be alone beside the [other note], but the note beside it not to a similar one [similis ante similem]. Also, that in some way it agrees in figure, even if not in name, with that which it can render imperfect, and that it be distinguished from it in the nearby genus, for example, if the imperfectible [note] has a quadrangular rectangular figure, then so [should] the imperfecting [note]. Also that the imperfecting [note] carries a certain part of the note which it has to imperfect.

Then let us see which things are required for a note to be perfectible by another, and for a note to perfect another. As for the first, it seems that a note which is perfectible by another must be imperfect, that is, not divisible into three equal parts, but rather into two, just as the [note] which is imperfectible must be in itself perfect and divisible into three equal parts. For what is it to be perfected if not to be turned from imperfect to perfect? For we are not speaking here of how something perfect may be brought to greater perfection. However, the single imperfect longa is imperfectible by any note whatsoever, any breve and semibreve both alike. And for the sake of brevity I leave off demonstrating more fully that no lone semibreve is capable, without another semibreve, of imperfecting or perfecting a note, because these things seem sufficiently clear from the things already said about them.

Accordingly there has been no need for the moderns to have labored so hard on those imperfections, and to multiply them in this way.

<Chapter 40. That one note may not imperfect another.>

Since *one should speak like many, but understand like few*, we have recounted some of the many things which they say about imperfections in musical notes. Now, however, let us consider which of those things would appear to be understandable as true. Now, unless I am mistaken, one note does not imperfect another [inasmuch] as [it is] a thing, as, for example, neither a breve nor a semibreve [imperfects] a longa or some other [note]. For that which does not act upon another [thing] does not imperfect it. And to imperfect is to act, because [it is] to turn perfect into imperfect. However, it does not seem that one musical note may act upon another because if it were to act, [it could only do so] through preternatural action (which nobody would say), or through natural action, or through voluntary [action].

Not through natural action, first, because natural action [is effected] through some kind of contact, for *that which does not touch does not act*; but one note does not seem to touch another. Second, because something which acts upon another in natural fashion, acts through an active potency which exists within it, just as that which suffers [the action of] another, suffers through a passive potency abiding within it; for an agent does not act upon just anything, but upon that which suffers [the action] and is disposed [to suffer it]. But one note does not seem to have active potency with respect to another, [nor does] another [have] passive [potency] with respect to the former. For mathematical things do not act, nor are they the principle of action, but this [thing] lacks active and passive qualities. For musical notes convey mathematical things such as continuous and discrete quantity. Also, it does not seem that one musical note acts upon another through voluntary action, because voluntary action is free with respect to the opposite. But an action of this sort does not pertain to the art.

From these things, therefore, and from other things that have been mentioned before or that could be mentioned, it seems that one musical note, [standing] beside another, can neither imperfect nor perfect it. And in order that these things may be more clearly apparent, let us respond to other arguments to the contrary.

<Chapter 41. Response to certain conclusions which contradict the things [we have] said.>

Yet there are some moderns who, approving of imperfections in notes, labor to demonstrate nine conclusions. The first is that a longa may be imperfected by a breve. Second, that a breve [may be imperfected] by a semibreve. Third, that a semibreve [may be imperfected] by a minim. Fourth, that a longa may be imperfected by a semibreve. Fifth, that a breve [may be imperfected] by a minim. Sixth, that a minim cannot be imperfected. Seventh, that an altera brevis cannot be imperfected by a semibreve. Eighth, that an altera semibrevis may be imperfected by a minim. Ninth, that tempus is divisible in as many equal parts as you like.

The first conclusion is demonstrated as follows. Every perfect thing [can be] reduced to an imperfect thing by having its third part taken away. For a perfect thing is divisible into three equal [parts], but an imperfect thing into two. Now the breve is the third part of a perfect longa through agents <which have thus divided it>. Hence the perfect longa is rendered imperfect by the breve, regardless of whether [that breve] be notated before or after. When a unity is taken from a ternary thing, in whatever way, there always remains an imperfect binary.

Before dealing with the arguments supporting other conclusions, let us respond to this, which seems to serve as the foundation for several others. Now it is to be noted here, first, that although the ancients commonly conceded the first conclusion, at least as far as manner of speaking is concerned, [they did] not [concede] the others. Nor is it to be imputed to them that they thought, somehow, that the breve acts in such way upon a perfect long that it imperfects it, meaning that it fashions an imperfect long out of that which was in truth perfect. Yet it remains to be explained how we are to understand the general premise that the breve imperfects the perfect long. When, therefore, it is said that every perfect thing is reduced to an imperfect thing by having its third part taken away, it must be said, firstly, that this "imperfect" seems to be [merely] an expression, since a perfect thing is not properly reduced to an imperfect thing, nor is the perfect properly born of the imperfect, not does it tend toward it, but rather the opposite.

It is to be stated, secondly, that when the third part of a perfect thing is taken away, and if it is of its essence, then is not so much imperfected as destroyed and corrupted—just as a house when [its] foundation, walls, or roof are removed; [or] the triangle, when one of the three lines or three angles [is removed]; or the ternary number, when the number one [is removed]. Similarly, if the third part of a perfect longa is taken away, then the latter is destroyed and [not] changed into an imperfect longa.

It is to be said, thirdly, that if the third part is taken away from continuous time, then the latter is not properly imperfected but rather diminished, just as when the third part is cut from a line which is divisible into three equal parts, [the line] is not imperfected on that account, but diminished, since the remaining [line] would be divisible into three equal or minor parts (just as the line itself [was] before). Thus also the longa of three equal tempora, if one is removed, remains the same according to the moderns, even according to this teacher in his ninth conclusion, as shall be apparent below.

Given that the breve supposedly had the power to imperfect a perfect longa (which is not to be conceded), it does not however follow that it would imperfect [that longa] when it would be beside it, for not every power is joined to its action. Not everything that can be generated is generated or shall be generated in future. I do not speak, however, of the immanent or formal act, such as to whiten with respect to whiteness, or to heat up with respect to heat, but of that which passes, which is to heat up with respect to the ability to be heated.

<Chapter 42. Response to the objection that could be raised.>

However, the objection will be raised against the things [we have] said, that if a breve beside a perfect long does not imperfect the latter, then such a long remains perfect after that addition. (But no one, it seems, has ever said this.)

Response: The lone breve, or that which is equivalent to it, is never placed beside a perfect longa, nor does it need it, but it is placed beside an imperfect longa in order that they together have three perfect tempora and thus fill out the perfect longa in value. And since the lone breve is not placed beside a perfect longa, it plainly does not imperfect the latter because, according to the authors, no note ever imperfects that which it is not beside to. It is also clear that a breve beside an imperfect long does not perfect it intrinsically, because [the long] is not in itself worth three tempora, but rather two, and the brevis [is worth] one, and thus the breve together with [the long] notates its posited meaning. Also, this is quite irrational, for a breve would have a depriving, destroying, and imperfecting significance beside a perfect longa, but a positive [significance] for the imperfect longa, and thus its meaning would vary between one case and another.

To understand the said general premise, namely, that a breve beside a long imperfects the latter, it is to be noted that the perfect and imperfect long agree with respect to figure. And in an equivocal sense, as seen above, one figure represents both this note and the other, and stands now for one of them, then for the other. And since equivocations are told apart by means of the things beside them, the authors have invented ways by which one can tell when the figure, which in an equivocal sense is common to both the perfect and imperfect longa, stands in a determinate sense for one or the other.

In this way, therefore, one can understand the general premise that the breve beside a long imperfects the latter, that is, it *shows* it to be imperfect in that location [but does not *make* it imperfect]. For this is one way in which the imperfect long is distinguished from the perfect long. For in this way it is made to signify according to its nature, when it is called imperfect and cannot stand by itself but needs beside it a lone breve, or semibreves that are equivalent to a lone breve. Yet the perfect longa, according to its nature and its name, can stand by itself. Therefore it has no need of a breve. Consequently there must never be a lone breve beside it, unless an imperfect longa were to be beside a recta brevis, or so many semibreves [beside it] as would be equivalent, together with that breve, to a perfect longa.

Nor does one ever find in the authors, at least not the ancient ones, that they claimed that a lone breve beside a perfect long would imperfect it. Yet they do say categorically that it "imperfects" a longa beside which it is notated because it *shows* it to be imperfect, that is, that it has a value of two tempora—not that it literally imperfects the perfect, and changes the imperfect. Like when the expression "dog" is taken equivocally for the barking animal, for the heavenly constellation [Canis major], for the marine fish [Mustelus canis]—not that the heavenly star was ever a barking dog, or a marine fish, [nor] that one of them may be changed into another. Thus the same figure is taken neither [exclusively] for the perfect nor for the imperfect longa—not that one of them could ever be converted into the other by placing some note beside them.

<Chapter 43. Response to the second conclusion, the fifth, sixth, seventh, and eighth.>

The response to the argument supporting the first conclusion is apparent from the things [we have] said. In which connection one should note this: although the first conclusion—understanding it, as already said, as a manner of speaking—is conceded both by the moderns and by some of the ancients (I say "some" because [Lambertus] did not use that manner of speaking), still the ancients did not posit the other conclusions, [and] they made no mention of them—for instance, that the semibreve could imperfect the breve, and the minim the major semibreve, and similarly about other things. For these [conclusions] present a different case from the first [conclusion], as is apparent from the things said above. For in them, the conditions that we have said are necessary for one note to imperfect another (in a manner of speaking rather than in actual fact) are lacking.

Therefore, if our response to the argument supporting the first conclusion has been that it is inconclusive, then so much more does it seem to be the proper response to the arguments supporting the other conclusions, since that conclusion seems more plausible than the others, and is conceded by several people, and the arguments [made] for the other conclusions are founded upon the argument supporting the afore-mentioned first conlusion. Therefore it suffices to go over them briefly.

Now when they say, with regard to the second and third conclusions: Every imperfection is effected through the taking-away of the third part, [and] the semibreve is the third part of the breve, and the minim the third part of the major semibreve, and so on, then we have already replied that it does not follow from this that the semibreve imperfects the breve, or the minim the major semibreve, just as the breve [does] not [imperfect] the perfect longa of which it is the third part. Neither is the case, here nor there, as we have seen.

The response to the argument sustaining the fourth conclusion, and the fifth, seventh, and eighth, is also apparent from the things [we have] said. For if the breve does not imperfect the perfect longa, [nor] the semibreve the breve, [nor] the minim the semibreve, then so much the less could a semibreve imperfect a perfect or imperfect longa, or an altera brevis, for the reasons mentioned already. The sixth conclusion, however, may be conceded, for if the perfect longa or any other note is not imperfectible, then [naturally] the minim is not either, Still, objections may be raised against the argument adduced in support of that conclusion, which I shall pass over.

<Chapter 44. Broader response to the things touching upon the fourth, seventh, and eighth conclusions, with a response to the ninth.>

Yet let us speak more fully of the things that touch upon the fourth, seventh, and eighth conclusions; and [proceeding] from there we shall respond to the ninth. Now, they say that the imperfect longa or altera brevis can be imperfected by the semibreve. This is not apparent, however, since, as already said, it is repugnant to imperfection to be imperfected; for it would lose its figure. Also, the imperfect, by definition, is not divisible into three equal parts. The aforesaid arguments add even more weight to this. Yet they say that imperfection is twofold; one is immediate (and the imperfect longa is not imperfected in that way), and the other mediate, which is brought about through the mediation of a part. They say, therefore, that since an imperfect longa worth [two] perfect tempora contains [two equal] parts that are in turn divisible into three equal parts, therefore it can be imperfected in [those latter] parts, because whatever imperfects a part also imperfects the whole.

Against this: First, a part, as part, is not imperfected for, as such, the rationale and divisibility of the whole is repugnant to it. Second, if the imperfect long were to be imperfected in its parts, that is, in the breves, then it would be imperfected by several imperfections, for its two parts are equal, and so it should be imperfected equally in one as well as in the other; therefore either in both or in neither. Third, since the breves are intrinsic to the rationale of that longa, then if that longa were to be imperfected in them, then the same thing in subject would act upon itself, since to imperfect is to act, as was deduced above, and the intrinsic part would destroy the whole. Fourth, action proceeds by contact, as said above. But things that are the same in subject do not touch one another. This is indicated also by the reasons mentioned before, from which it is apparent that an integral whole is not only not imperfected in its intrinsic and essential parts, or in some one of them, but is preserved in its being.

Yet let us come to the ninth conclusion, which is that tempus may be divided in however many parts you like. It must be said that although tempus, taken materially and absolutely, may be divided like a continuum in as many equal parts as you like, as in two, three, four, and so on, [tempus] as signified by musical notes [may] not [be so divided], as has been pointed out repeatedly. For it is one thing to be divisible as designated by a perfect long, and another by an imperfect one. For all notes convey determinate stretches of time, and are distinguished from each other in this respect, yet they generally agree on this point that they convey tempus in the same way as the year, the month, the day, the quarter, the hours, the moment, the twelfth part, the atom. Also, musical notes do not seem to convey purely continuous time, but discrete and numbered time applicable or applied to determinate parts, as demonstrated above, and as confirmed by the moderns, even by the [teacher] who posits those nine conclusions.

Now, however, we must devote some attention to the things he says in the ninth conclusion: Every continuum, he says, is divisible in as many parts of the same proportion as you like, as in twos or in threes or in fours, and so on. Tempus is [classed] among things that are continuous. Therefore it can be divided in as many equal parts as you like. And therefore song could be made from two, three, four, five, six, seven, eight, nine, equal semibreves of the same figure, and so on.

Yet one should note that the ancients, following the art of Franco, have used more distinctions between semibreves as far as the thing itself [rather than the name] is concerned, than the moderns. For the latter seem never to use four semibreves for one recta brevis, never five or seven or eight, like the ancients have done. And when the moderns say that a praiseworthy and skilled musician could sing upon the same equal tempus now three, now four semibreves, now five, six, seven, eight, or nine, then according to [their own statement] it is the old who should be commended, given that the ancients actually did this, as is apparent from the examples given above, but the moderns never did.

And now, towards the end of this burdensome work to which we have devoted so much, let us draw, after the manner which we observed above in some places, some comparisons between the old art of measurable music and the modern, in order that we may also repond more fully to some of the things which the moderns say against the ancients.

<Chapter 45. Comparison of the ancient art of measurable music to the new as far as perfection and imperfection are concerned.>

Here, towards the end of this work, let us offer some comparisons drawn from the aforesaid things. And let not some be indignant at this. I have spoken without any prejudice whatsoever, and I say the things as they appear to me. To accept or reject [them] on account of [my person] does not change anything about the matter itself. Let that be upheld which obeys reason or greater reason, and which is more consonant with this art; let that be rejected which is of less. For since man lives by art and reason, there must be a place within any man for that which is reason and that which is art. Reason follows the law of nature which God has distributed in rational creatures.

Now since we have spoken lastly about imperfections, in order that these matters be continued, let the first comparison between the ancient art of measurable music and the modern be according to perfection and imperfection.

Perhaps it seems to some that the modern art is more perfect than the old, because it seems more subtle and difficult. More subtle because it encompasses many things, and adds many things to [the old], as is apparent in the notes, in the modes and measures (though we call "subtle" that which is more incisive, probing into many things). And that which is more difficult can be seen in the works of the moderns, in the manner of singing and measuring.

To others, however, it seems the other way round, because that art must seem more perfect which follows its foundation more closely and goes against it less. For the art of measurable music is founded in perfection, as say not only the old but the moderns as well. Therefore, that which makes greater use of perfect things seems more perfect. And this is the case with the ancient art, the art of Magister Franco.

But the new art, as already seen, uses manifold and varyious imperfections, in notes, in modes, in measures. Imperfection creeps in almost everywhere, nor is imperfection in notes, or modes, or measures, sufficient to [that art], but it extends [imperfection] even to tempus. For the new art posits imperfect tempus, and [it posits] breves under this name "imperfect," with respect to tempus, [things] which the old art has never posited. And it applies the imperfection which comes from tempus to single notes of [several] degrees: to single longas, duplex or even triplex [longas], to breves, and some to semibreves.

Now those using the new art invent new ways in which they can imperfect what is perfect, even by multiple imperfections, through close or immediate [notes], like when the single perfect longa is imperfected by a breve; by distant [notes] when the same [longa] is imperfect by a semibreve, because [the semibreve] is the third part the recta brevis; and more distant when the same longa is imperfected by a minim. Nor is it sufficient for the moderns to imperfect things that are perfect, and to drag them into imperfection, on the contrary—imperfect things as well, as if one imperfect thing were not sufficient, but [there should be] several.

Now if the new art were to speak of the said imperfections only in speculative fashion, it would be more tolerable. But that is not the case. For they greatly extend imperfection to practice; they use more imperfect things than perfects; more imperfect modes than perfect ones, and consquently measures as well.

So when they say: the new art is more subtle than the ancient, then even if that is conceded, it does not follow that it is also more perfect. For not every subtle thing can claim perfection, nor [can] greater subtlety [claim] greater perfection. *Subtlety is not posited among the degrees or species of perfection*, as is evident in the <fourth book> of Metaphysics.

Nor has it been sufficiently demonstrated that the new art is more subtle than the ancient, given that the latter contains things which are not contained in the new. The fact that [the new art] contains many imperfections which are not contained in the old art does not imply that it is more perfect; but it does raise the question, as a consequence, which of the said arts is more perfect.

But [with regard to] what is said after that, namely, that the modern art is more difficult that the ancient, it must be replied that it does not follow from this that it is also more perfect. For that which is more difficult is not, simply speaking, more perfect. For although art may be said to be about what is difficult, it actually is about what is good and useful, since [art] is the power to perfect the soul through the mediation of the intellect. Whence [scriptural] authority says that *knowledge is easy unto him that understandeth*. But let us deal with that below.

<Chapter 46. Comparison of the old art of measurable music to the modern according to subtletly and crudeness.>

Some moderns consider those singers crude, dim-witted, foolish, and ignorant who do not know the new art, or who do not sing according to [that art] but according to the ancient. And they consequently consider the ancient art crude and almost irrational, yet the new subtle and rational.

Yet it may be asked from where moderns have acquired that subtlety, and ancients that crudeness. For if subtlety comes from a greater and more incisive mind, then who are to be reckoned the more subtle? Those who have discovered the principles against which [the moderns] have acted, but who observed those things almost to a hair? Or these who profess that they will observe those principles, yet who do not observe them but rather seem to fight against them?

Let this be considered by wise men who may bring true judgement without bias. And what is the value of subtlety, what [the value] of difficulty, when utility is lost? What is the value of such subtlety as obstructs the principles of science? Are the subtlety and difficulty which of those many and various imperfections [that have been] invented in notes, tempora, modes, and measures, not unsuited to that science which is founded in perfection? Is this not to indulge in imperfections of great subtlety, and to do away with perfections? Must the ancients be called crude because they have used perfect things, and the moderns subtle because [they use] imperfect things? Must the moderns be called subtle because they invent triplex longas, ligate duplex longas, notate duple longas [called] largas, that they notate lone semibreves, that they caudate them, that they give them the power to imperfect longas and breves, and one another, [all of] which do not seem necessary to his art, and many other things which they posit and which seem to be repugnant to the art by reason of its foundation?

Must they be called subtle because of their new manner of singing in which the words are lost, the effect of good concord is diminished, and the measure is confused, as will be mentioned below? And who are the ones who use many different songs and manners of singing, and who apply themselves to many different songs and manners of singing? Do not the moderns practice almost nothing but motets and songs, except when they insert hockets in their motets? Yet they reject many other songs which they do not use in their proper form, like the ancients did, such as organal songs that are [fully] measured or [partially] measured, like organum purum or duplum, of which few of the moderns have perhaps any knowledge; also conducti, songs of such beauty, in which there is so much delight, which are so artful and delightful, duplex, triplex, and quadruplex ones: and also hockets, likewise duplex, contraduplex, triplex, and quadruplex ones. The ancient singers devoted themselves alternately to each of these, in these they sought their foundation, in these they practised, in these they delighted, not just in motets or songs alone.

Should one call crude, dim-witted, and ignorant in the art of singing those men who knew (or know) those songs, and who made (or make) use of them, just because they do not sing the modern songs, or [sing] according to the manner of the moderns, and do not use the new art of the moderns? They would know that [art] if they wanted to set their hearts to it and to sing according to the modern manner. Yet it does not please them. Rather the ancient [manner pleases them], perhaps because of the things that have been mentioned before, or that could be mentioned.

One modern teacher speaks thus: *The duplex long in perfect modus is worth six tempora, when it should truly be worth nine; and in this regard Franco and Petrus de Cruce and all the others are in error.*

This teacher seems to berate not just the ancient teachers, of whom he mentions two very distinguished ones by name, but also the moderns, since he says in this statement that it is not just those two who are in error, but "all the others." He does not say "the ancients," but rather says categorically "all the others," and consequently [includes] himself as well, since he is one of them, too. And if they are all crude in what they have erred in, [and] in this statement he deems them all crude, then this teacher seems to be speaking without civility. Let him take heed lest he be even more in error in this statement, to which we have responded above, and in certain others of his abovementioned statements. But I think that he believed to be speaking truth, just like the other teachers.

Yet the ancient art must not be deemed crude and irrational, it seems, not only because the things opposing it, or some of the additions by the moderns, have been shown earlier to be irrational or not necessary to the art, but also because, even if the moderns have added many good things to the ancient art, it does not follow from this that [the latter], and its inventors and those using it, are therefore crude and irrational. Although many good things have been added to the art of tones or modes which Boethius handed down to us, by teachers that came after him such as Guido the monk and others, for that reason the art of Boethius, and Boethius himself, must not be deemed irrational and crude. For he laid the foundations of the art, laid down principles from which others following him extracted good and useful conclusions that are consonant with the art, not things contrary to those principles, not repugnant to them.

And if the moderns use many distinctions, many denominations, for semibreves, at least with regard to the figures, it seems that the ancients use many things rather with regard to the thing itself, as we have mentioned. Now if they were able to notate, for the same and equal tempus carried [by] the recta brevis, now two unequal semibreves, now three equal ones, now four, now five, six, seven, eight, or nine, then whenever they notated two, they could have called those semibreves *secundae*, because two of them rendered that breve; and when three semibreves, *tertiae*, because three of them were equal in value to a breve; when four semibreves, *quartae* for the said reason; when five semibreves, *quintae*; when six semibreves, *sextae*; when seven semibreves, *septimae*; when eight semibreves, *octavae*; when nine semibreves, *nonae* (as we have said above). Although they used so many distinctions between semibreves, they never caudated them and yet they divided them adequately by means of dots.

<Chapter 47. Comparison of the ancient measurable art to the new with regard to freedom and servitude.

The art of singing of the moderns seems to be compare to the ancient [art] as a mistress to a servant or handmaid. For the new art seems now to govern, and the ancient [art] to act as handmaid. The new art rules, the ancient art lives in exile. But is this reasonable, that the one which uses perfect things should be subordinated, and that [which uses] imperfect things should govern, when the more perfect should be lord rather than servant? For those [two] arts seem to compare to one another as the Old Law to the New, except that in this comparison the art of the moderns seems to have the condition of the Old Law, and the ancient art that of the New. For the New Law is more perfect, more free, more uncomplicated, and more easy to fulfill than the Old; for the New Law contains fewer precepts, [and these are] light to fulfil. Whence the Lord [says] in the Gospel: *For my yoke is easy and my burden is light.* And the blessed James in his canonic epistle: *If anyone has looked into the law of perfect freedom.*

Now the Old Law contained many and diverse moral, judicial, and ceremonial precepts which were difficult to fulfill. Whence the blessed Peter, speaking about the Old Law, says in the Acts of the Apostles: *Now therefore why tempt ye God, to put a yoke upon the neck of the disciples, which neither our fathers nor we were able to bear?*

The ancient measurable art contains few and clear teachings compared to the modern [art]. But the moderns use [many] precepts in their various longs, breves, and semibreves, in their various manners and measures of singing, they posit various teachings for the making of imperfect things, they use [many] rules for the discerning of songs. It would take a long time to render a full account, nor are they fully in agreement about [their] teachings.

For some notate in [their] songs a round circle to designate *tempus perfectum*, since the round form is perfect, as here:

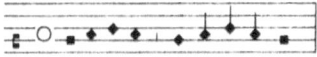

Others however notate three little strokes to designate the same, as here:

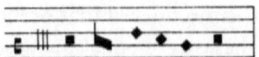

And those three little strokes must touch a line and [also] a little of the space on either side, in order that those little strokes be thus distinguished from the things they call rests. And he who posits this doctrine greatly rebukes those who have no knowledge of it, holding them to be mentally deficient and foolish, for here lies great science and great wisdom (and let those be positive things). And tempus perfectum and imperfectum, if they are to be notated, can be distinguished from each another in another way, or many other ways, than those.

For the indication of perfect modus, however, they notate a quadrangle which contains three little dashes, as here:

And for the designation of imperfect modus, they notate a quadrangle which contains two little dashes, in the manner which follows:

Others, on the other hand, place a sign of two half-circles to designate imperfect [modus], thus:

and by that sign they denote both tempus and modus; and, as a certain other man says: *They cannot indicate one of them without the other.*

Others take it upon themselves to add an M for perfect modus, and N for imperfect, saying that just as O and C are notated for changes in tempus, so M and N [are notated] for knowledge of the modus. Others, however, almost in opposition, understand by O the perfect mode and perfect measure; but by C, the imperfect modus and imperfect measure. Others say that for perfect tempus and modus one may place a circle containing within itself three little strokes, as is apparent here:

Yet for the designation of imperfect tempus and modus they write a semicircle containing within itself two little strokes, as here:

The moderns notate these and many other things which the ancients never notated, and in this way they place many burdens on the art, which was formerly free from those burdens, and wich would now seem to be a slave with regard to these things.

Now although, according to Seneca, freedom is about the greatest goods (whence the poetic [saying]: *freedom is not well sold for all the gold* [in the world]), and although the ancient art is free from such burdens, still the moderns do not permit [the latter] to reign. Now, since there is no satisfactory government when a free person who ought to be lord cannot act out of free [will], Aristotle very much rejects such dominion or rule in his Politics.

<Chapter 48. Comparison of the old art of measurable music to the modern, and the ancient manner of singing to the modern, with regard to stability.>

One distinction, among others, between a perfect work and an imperfect one is that the perfect work is more stable than the imperfect. For that which is perfect has no need of something else, is not arranged to accommodate something else. That which is perfect has a good foundation. Therefore, whichever of the two measurable arts is more perfect, that is, the old or the modern, must also be more stable.

Now, we see sometimes, as mentioned above, that new teachings are unstable, because although they may be received joyfully and freely at first, on account of their novelty, yet afterwards, when they have been examined well, and [are found to be] lacking solid foundations, they displease and are cast away, and people return to the more ancient teachings.

If only this were the case with the modern measurable art compared to the old one. For since the modern teachers do not quite agree on the said art in their treatises, this is a sign of the instability of their art. For it is written: *Every reign divided against itself is brought to desolation.* Now if one opposes the other, how shall their reign stand? Accordingly division heralds evil and instability, according to what the prophet Hosea wrote: *Their heart is divided; now shall they be found faulty.*

Measurable music moreover needs concord and flees away from discord. In this regard, therefore, it does not ask for discordant teachers; but all things are consonant with the true and good.

If only it would please modern singers to bring the ancient art, the ancient songs and manner of singing, back into use. For if I may say so, the old art seems more perfect, more free, more reasonable, more respectable, more simple, and more plain.

Have not the moderns turned music, which was so sensible in its beginning, so respectable, simple, manly, and well regulated, into something too wanton? By doing so they have offended, and still offend, many wise men who are skilled in music, just as <Timotheus> Milesius offended the Spartans or Laconians, as mentioned in the first book.

Let wise men pay attention and judge what is true.

Why has the use of the old art been banished, and [also] the song of the ancients and the manner of singing, for the sake of the modern [songs] and the manner of singing of the moderns? How could they have deserved this? What could they have done? Have they not been banished because they are good and yet do not please the satraps, like King Achis said of David: *thou hast been upright . . . nevertheless the lords favour thee not*? It is unlawful that anyone should be exiled from his homeland unless for a certain and just reason, or that he be excluded from the fellowship of the faithful like an excommunicate unless because of his demerit.

By all this I do not mean to say that the moderns have not made beautiful and good songs. But the ancients should not be called bad for that reason, or be excluded from the fellowship of singers. One good thing is not the enemy of another.

I have seen distinguished singers and knowledgeable laymen in a certain society where they had come together. There, modern motets were sung according to the modern manner, and also some old ones. The ancient ones were much more pleasing, even to the laymen, than the new ones, and the ancient manner [much more] than the new. For although the new manner pleased by its novelty, it is not thus now, but [rather] it begins to displease many. Therefore it would be pleasing to bring the ancient songs and the ancient manner of singing and notation, back to the homeland of singers. Let them be restored to use, and let rational art flourish once more. It lived in exile, and so did its manner of singing. Almost violently have they been cast out from the fellowship of singers. *But what is violent must not be everlasting.*

Why is this wantonness of singing so pleasing? [Why] this curiosity in which, as it seems to some, the words are lost, the harmony of consonances is diminished, the value of notes is changed, perfection cast down, imperfection raised up, and the measure confused?

I have witnessed, when motets were sung according to the modern manner, in a great society of wise men, that people asked what sort of language the singers were using: Hebrew, Greek or Latin, or some other, because it could not be understood what they said. Thus, although the moderns may write many beautiful and good texts in their songs, they lose them in their manner of singing, when these are not understood.

These are the things which it occurred to me to say in affirmation of the old measurable art and in defense of those who have used it. And because I have not found other teachers before me who would write about this matter, I hope that I shall find supporters who shall be willing to write about this, and fortify it with better reasons than the ones given here.

<Chapter 49. Final conclusion of this whole work, and thanksgiving.>

Thus have I labored up to now in explaining music as faithfully as I could, theoretical as well as practical, plain and measurable, generally and specifically, now together, now separately. But now there is an end to my enquiring any further into the same [art]. Let other more subtle minds step forward, lovers of this noble science who, if they wish to study it diligently and attentively to deepen [their knowledge] of it, as it requires, shall be able to elicit and write about many things which still lie hidden within its principles.

Yet what do I speak, weak and insignificant man who have written these things? For just as the Blessed Job says: *One thing have I said which I would I had not said, and also another thing, [but] I will not add more to these*, so I, when I wanted to revise and emend, in looking over this entire work, one or another thing I had written, found not just one thing and another, that is, two, but many things which I wish I had not said, or had said differently. But I have said that which occurred to me then, and what seemed true to me then. For not just do different people understand different things, as [there are] so many heads and so many wits; but also in different times one understands now this way, now in another, now this occurs, now some other thing.

And if I had always kept changing things, when would I have reached the end of this work? Perhaps never. And although choice should be about what is better, yet there are many things that occur there, and not always is that chosen which is better or more true. For reason in us is deficient, and choice deficient. Where I have been deficient, I plead, let it be corrected or be taken as not said. This favor I beg, I entreat, to be conceded to me. For it is indeed written: *We may speak much, and yet come short: wherefore in sum, he is all.* And according to Priscian: *In human affairs nothing is perfect.* And according to that [saying] by Cicero: *nature has made nothing of any genus absolutely perfect in all parts, as if there would be nothing to bestow on others if it had given everything to one.*

For this reason I adopt for my person that which Boethius said at the end of his book on the two natures and the one person in Christ, where he speaks thus: *if I have said aught amiss, I am not so well pleased with myself as to try to press my effusions in the face of wiser judgment. For if there is no good thing in us there is nothing we should fancy in our opinions. But if all things are good as coming from Him who alone is good, that rather must be thought good which the Unchangeable Good and Cause of all Good indites.* Because of the things that have been said and that could be said, let them make, I pray, . . . in excusation of my shortcomings—the length of this work, the labor and solicitude, the dullness of my wit, the subtlety, variety, and diversity of the matter, and the fragility of [my] age.

Oh, how many times, having lingered in the many difficult passages, have I considered, and considered again, the Muse, as in the many specific proportions of many consonances that are to be found, and their first or least numbers, in the appropriate figures to be used, in the demonstrations to be made in their [proper] places, in explaining Boethius in many places, in arranging the chapters of this work, in continuing this matter and pondering what I would say next and next and how! Oh how many times have I interrupted this work for some time! And since music requires a man who is not distracted from treating it, yet would wish to have him all [to herself], I, [having been] often distracted, returned to continue this work only [as a] more awkward, more crude, and slow [man], for which reason it has taken much more time. I have however preferred to be clear rather than obscure in this work; for a mirror must be clear, not obscure, and I have chosen that it would not lack an expositor. Have I not used a simple style, very plain and bare?

Blessed be God for ever, through whose power, through whose benevolent will, I have undertaken this work, continued it, and have brought it to an end. He is the first and highest Good from which all secondary goodness flows, he is the first, pure, uncreated, Truth from whom all secondary truth is born. Therefore I render such thanks as I am able to, not as I owe. Glory, praise, honor, reverence, majesty, holiness to Him. Whatever reverence it is open to say and think, I praise, honor, and bless him as much as I have the strength to do.

Yet although [my abilities] do not suffice properly to render thanks to God for this and other blessings granted to me, [and although] this mortal life does not suffice for that either, nor [all] the sounding music of this world, even though the [musical] instrument is said to be for the praise of God, I ask suppliantly that all who have seen this work, however many, to whom I recommend myself, may deign to intercede for me, the compiler. May the Rewarder and Doer of all good, through his mercy after the end of this wretched life, consider me worthy to be led to the perfect state of those heavenly denizens in the company of all good humans, who devote themselves to that most perfect music, namely, the heavenly or divine [music mentioned] above, by which I, together with those denizens, would bless, glorify, and magnify God incessantly, continuously, and most intently, where I would see him, as he is, intuitively, would delight in him, would love him with consummate charity, would always have him favorably inclined and near me, where I would never offend him, never commit a sin, since I would find whatever I could desire, from which state I would never fall, in eternity, through our most excellent Lord Jesus Christ who together with the Father and the Holy Ghost lives and reigns, one and only true God, blessed for ages of ages.

Amen.

Here ends [The Mirror of Music].

www.ingramcontent.com/pod-product-compliance
Lightning Source LLC
Chambersburg PA
CBHW031644170426
43195CB00035B/576